The Lord Is My Shepherd

and I'm About to be SHEARED!

The Lord Is My Shepherd

and I'm About to be

SHEARED!

G. Ron Darbee

BROADMAN & HOLMAN PUBLISHERS

Nashville, Tennessee

0-8054-6358-5

Published by Broadman & Holman Publishers,
Nashville, Tennessee
Page compositor: R. R. Donnelley & Sons
Acquisitions Editor: Vicki Crumpton

Dewey Decimal Classification: 234.4
Subject Heading: CHRISTIAN LIFE—HUMOR
Library of Congress Card Catalog Number: 97-48476

Unless otherwise noted all Scripture quotations are from the
New International Version, copyright © 1973, 1978, 1984 by
International Bible Society. Scripture quotations marked (NKJV)
are from the New King James Version, copyright © 1979, 1980,
1982, Thomas Nelson, Inc., Publishers.

Library of Congress Cataloging-in-Publication Data
Darbee, G. Ron. 1961–
    The Lord is my shepherd and I'm about to be sheared /
G. Ron Darbee.
        p.   cm.
    ISBN 0-8054-6358-5 (pbk.)
    1. Christian life—Humor.   2. Christian life—Anecdotes.
I. Title.
BV4517.D366   1998
243.4'02'07—dc21   97-48476
                                                        CIP

1 2 3 4 5 02 01 00 99 98

Care to comment to the author?
G. Ron Darbee can be reached via E-mail at
DarbeeGR@aol.com

DEDICATION

This book is dedicated to my parents,
 Ronald R. and Mary Elizabeth Darbee,
 with much love and gratitude for
 their example of unconditional love.

CONTENTS

ACKNOWLEDGMENTS

Once again, I find myself extremely grateful for the many friends and family members who have offered their encouragement and support. God continues to bless us with people who give their love freely and in abundance. For this I give thanks.

To my wife, Sue. Thank you for providing the balance our home and family needs. Your partnership in this effort is as evident as it is in every accomplishment of our lives. I praise God that he gave us each to the other.

Ron, you are the son every father hopes for and not the one your grandmother said I deserved. I appreciate your wit and humor and the special friendship we share.

Melissa, you are and will always be my darling. Your kindness and infectious enthusiasm keep us all smiling.

To pastors Craig Stonehocker and Bill Barnett: Thanks for your patience and friendship. You have given me a wonderful example of how God can take a difficult situation and use it to his benefit. Pastors Dave Harris, Glen Evans, and Dave Malouf, thank you for your service.

Sincere thanks to the Broadman & Holman publishing family for their partnership in this book. To Vicki Crumpton, my editor and friend, thank you for your patience, flexibility, and unending support. Mark Lusk, thank you for believing in this project and encouraging me along the way. Rene Holt, thanks for poor judgment in making authors your friends. I still say Waffle House is among the finest restaurants in the South. My appreciation to the folk from sales for making a reluctant speaker feel at home and welcome. To everyone at Broadman & Holman, thank you for working with me and allowing me to be a part of your team.

To all of our friends who prayed and praised God alongside us: thank you so very much. And Joe Wickham, could I really have done this without you?

CHAPTER 1

The Lord Is My Shepherd and I'm About to Be Sheared

When my children were very young, I loved to read to them the story of *The Little Engine That Could*. My father read it to me as a child, and his father read it to him. It's an old story; a classic passed down from generation to generation with many variations in print. I imagine Adam read a version to Abel, but probably not to Cain—I don't think he spent enough time with Cain.

I still remember sitting on my father's lap listening to the *Puff! Chug! Squeak! Sque-e-e-ak!* of that little engine as it tried and tried to climb the mountain and deliver Christmas toys to children living in the village beyond. *Puff! Chug! Squeak! Sque-e-e-ak!* The little engine made run after run at the base of that mountain, but try as he might, he never made it up the grade;

1

that is, until Norman Vincent Peale got hold of him and gave the little engine a copy of *The Power of Positive Thinking* (like I said, there are several variations of the story). The diminutive locomotive, now empowered with a positive attitude, changed his motto from, "Man that's one steep mountain," to, "I think I can, I think I can" and charged forward one more time.

Now, had he really paid attention to the book, his motto would have been, "I know I can, I know I can," but I guess one has to crawl before one can walk, and in this case, "I think I can" proved good enough. The little engine set his mind on an objective, thought positively, and completed the task at hand. With a *Puff! Chug! Squeak! Sque-e-e-ak!*—chanting all the while, "I think I can, I think I can," the engine climbed right up the side of that mountain, reached the peak, and cruised effortlessly down the other side with his cargo of Christmas toys. Success!

The children in the village were happy. The little engine was overjoyed. Everyone in the whole wide world was just ecstatic because this train overcame adversity, reached deep down inside, and gutted it out. The children received their Christmas toys, and the little engine went on to bigger and better things, hauling movie stars around the Hollywood hills. He eventually retired to Orlando where he occasionally makes an appearance at Disney World, schlepping kids around. Most importantly, everybody lived happily ever after. Yeah, right.

Somewhere along the line, shortly after I went out on my own and long before my first mid-life crisis, I adopted this story as my own. I became the little engine and took his motto as my life's credo: "I think I can, I think I can." This attitude permeated everything I did and everything I wanted to accomplish. I can do it! It's not a matter of *if:* it's all about *when.* Tell me what you want, and let me figure out how. Some people call it drive or determination, but there is another word for it too.

I bought all of the books, and I actually read most of them. I became the *One-Minute Manager* and practiced a majority of the *Seven Habits of Highly Effective People*. If asked, *What Color is Your Parachute?* I provided a weighty and meaningful answer. I Puffed! Chugged! Squeaked! Sque-e-e-aked! toward whatever I deemed as the goal of the moment, all the while chanting, "I think I can, I think I can." And for a while, I did.

"Staff Sergeant Darbee, there's been a spill out at the fuel farm. Can you take care of it?" *What do I know about cleaning up 50,000 gallons of jet fuel?* I think I can, I think I can.

"Are you really ready to take on the responsibilities of a husband? a father?" I think I can, I think I can.

"We need someone in Youth Ministries . . ." I think I can, I think I can.

"Take this proposal home over the weekend, and let me know what you think." I think I can, I think I can.

Men's discipleship—I think I can . . .

A church paper—I think I can . . .

Soccer, basketball, and little league tournaments—I think . . . no, wait a minute, I can't. I just can't do it anymore.

That realization snuck up on me. It came gradually over a period of months, and I was forced to admit that I can't do everything. I took it as a sign of failure, an inadequacy, or a flaw in my character. "I think I can" became "Maybe I can't," and the mountain loomed larger and steeper than ever. As ridiculous as it seems, for me—as with many goal-oriented people—I fell into the trap of believing that if I can't do everything, I probably can't do anything.

Work became a drudgery, and home just a place to pass the time. The alarm clock sounded every morning, and with it came an uneasiness like a lump in the pit of my stomach. *Go through the motions, just go through the motions*, I told myself time and again. *Get through this day so you can go home and sit in front of the television set until it's time to go to sleep. No more discipleship or service to my church. Please don't expect anything from me, family. I bring home a paycheck, isn't that enough? I can't be everything to everyone anymore. I can't do it all. For crying out loud, I'm not—*

Wait a minute. I'm not who? God? I'm not God? No, I'm not God. I am not God, and I am not supposed to be everything to everyone. Who put that requirement on me anyway? The answer came easily; I put it on myself. Sure, I could try to blame our culture or society's expectations. Maybe I could have drawn a line back to my father's lap and the story of *The Little Engine That Could* and laid a little guilt at his feet. But the truth of the matter is that I have no one to blame but myself.

It all comes down to a word I alluded to earlier: a synonym for *drive* and *determination*. It's *pride*. We all face battles with pride to one degree or another. Pride is charging forward without consulting God. (It's just a minor decision, after all. No sense bothering the Big Guy with this one.) Pride is believing that we have the ability to accomplish anything without God's help. Pride is self-determination, self-reliance, and self-rule. Pride is the sin of self, and I had it in shovelfuls.

It reminds me of a sheep farm nearby—or maybe it's a sheep ranch. I'm originally from New York and not expected to know such things. Either way, this guy owns a lot of sheep and a lot of land. I rode out there and looked around during shearing season. What I learned—besides the fact that sheep smell really bad, and you have to watch where you step—helped me understand something about my own purpose.

Most of the year, sheep wander around aimlessly, doing things that sheep do well. I'm not exactly sure what that is, but it involves eating grass and generally loitering about the property; they seem content with this, and so does the farmer/rancher. However, come shearing time, happiness blows away like the wind. The farmer/rancher herds them all together and begins singling them out, one by one. Ranch hands lock the woolly buggers into contraptions built to immobilize them, and commence with shaving them down until they resemble large, ugly dogs. Sheep, known for their vanity, hate looking like big ugly dogs, and therefore despise the shearing process. They put up a huge fuss—kicking, squirming, and bleating loudly until they are released; some even protesting a while longer.

The interesting thing to me is that the shearing process really benefits the sheep. Even though they don't enjoy it, shearing allows the sheep to fulfill their purpose—in this case, making money for the farmer/rancher. Yes, it's uncomfortable and maybe a little scary, but it doesn't hurt the sheep, and without it their prospects look pretty dismal. Let's face it, sheep make lousy pets, and if they don't meet the rancher's needs by providing wool, their only other value involves mint jelly—not the alternative of choice.

I've come to look at failure in much the same way. From time to time, God allows me to experience defeat. I don't believe he causes my failure; I do that well enough on my own, thank you very much. But in the midst of it all, God is there to remind me that I need to depend on him. When I fall short, I fall short because I set my own goals or tried to accomplish too much on my own—I have relied on my abilities rather than on him. And when I fail, I usually put up a fuss—kicking, squirming, and bleating my dissatisfaction—often for some time to come. Then I remember that I'm not the little engine that could.

Success is fun. Success is easy to deal with. But when I get too comfortable in my success and begin to pat myself on the back for my accomplishments, I try to remember that the Lord is my Shepherd, and I'm about to be sheared. If I've learned anything about success, it is that failure looms right around the corner. That's OK. Failure is good too. We learn a lot more from our failures than we ever glean from success.

My kids have grown too old to listen to stories on my knee, but someday we may have grandchildren running around the house. And if we do, I'll sit them down on my lap and tell them stories until they can't sit still any longer. I'll tell them about how the little engine *Puffed! Chugged! Squeaked!* and *Sque-e-e-aked!* at the base of that mountain, how he tried and tried, but how, eventually, they off-loaded the cargo onto a larger train because there are some things you just can't do by yourself. I hope they like it. I know I will.

The LORD is my shepherd, I shall not be in want. He makes me lie

down in green pastures, he leads me beside quiet waters, he restores my

soul. He guides me in paths of righteousness for his name's sake. Even

though I walk through the valley of the shadow of death, I will fear no

evil, for you are with me; your rod and your staff, they comfort me. You

prepare a table before me in the presence of my enemies. You anoint my

head with oil; my cup overflows. Surely goodness and love will follow me

all the days of my life, and I will dwell in the house of the LORD forever.

Psalm 23

CHAPTER 2

The Game of Life

"Ron, do you have something you'd like to say for yourself?" I asked the question with the entire family assembled. It was several years ago, and Sue was sitting on the couch comforting a distraught Melissa. I was leaning forward in my recliner, and my son Ron stood in the doorway surveying the mood of the room. From all appearances, he was trying hard to remember which of his recent escapades might have led to this unpleasant inquisition. "If you do," I suggested, "this would be a good time to speak up."

"I'm sorry?" Though he chose the correct words, the questioning inflection made me doubt his sincerity.

"Ding—Ding—Ding! Good answer. Good answer!" I applauded like a contestant on a game show we used to watch, then sat quietly, waiting for my son to elaborate on his apology. I was hoping for something resembling a confession of guilt, but soon determined that would be a long time coming.

"Is that it?" he asked, turning toward the kitchen, ready to make a hasty retreat.

"Oh, I don't think so," I answered. "The game's just beginning. Care to explain what you're sorry for?" This is a tactic I employed quite successfully when the kids were younger, often receiving admissions of guilt for transgressions of which I was not yet aware. But over the years they've learned the ins and outs of our parenting techniques, and don't often fall for that approach anymore.

Ron looked around the room again, wisely coming to focus on the image of his sister sniffling and crying on her mother's shoulder. I believe I witnessed the moment of revelation: his eyebrows twitched momentarily, and his jaw clenched shut as his mind pinpointed the probable cause of this most recent summoning. Still, he pleaded the fifth.

"No, but if I did it, I'm sorry."

"Well, Son," I said, "knowing how difficult it is for a creative guy like yourself to keep track of the many events and circumstances life throws your way, I brought along a few visual aids that might serve to trigger your memory. Would you like to see them?"

"I don't think so," Ron said.

"Ehhhhhh," I tried my best to imitate a game show buzzer. "Wrong answer, Son. Let's give it a try, anyway."

Ron shuffled his feet and stared deep into the carpet below, not appearing the least bit enthusiastic about the upcoming presentation of evidence.

"Item number one," I said, pulling a piece of paper from the end table next to my chair and holding it up for display. "This is a birth certificate, and if it pleases the judges"—I looked to my wife and daughter as I continued—"I wish to point out the doctor's signature and the official seal of the state of New York."

Ron glanced up at it momentarily before returning to his inspection of the carpet. I thought I detected the beginnings of a smile on his face, which was confirmation enough—as if I needed it. He appeared to be gnawing on the inside of his cheek, evidently trying to force the grin away.

"Aside from the seal," I continued, "and the high quality paper, the names, the dates, and the official-looking signatures, I have other reasons to believe this document is genuine. Care to know what they are?"

"No?" Again, the boy's inflection was off, and I felt compelled to give him the buzzer.

"Ehhhhhh!"

Melissa, no longer sniffling, appeared to be enjoying herself; Ron, not so much. "I know it's a bit late to explain the rules of our game, Ron, but it is my game. Here are the rules: The pleasant sounding ding signifies a correct answer. The unpleasant buzzer sound, Ehhhhhh," I demonstrated it again for effect, "denotes an incorrect answer. Three incorrect answers—you have already accumulated two—wins you an all-expense paid trip to nowhere for the next two weeks. You'll enjoy no phone calls, no computer time, no Nintendo, and as a specially added bonus, the sponsors have agreed to throw in no allowance. The total value of cash and prizes comes to . . . let me check my figures . . . nothing! We call this our Wrath-of-Dad Package."

By this time Ron was trying very hard not to laugh and failing miserably. He knew he was in deep trouble, I knew he was in deep trouble, the neighbors probably had a clue, but we were enjoying ourselves, so why not make discipline fun?

"What do I get if I win?" Ron asked.

"You won't, Son; trust me on this."

"Well, if I can't win, I'm not playing."

"Yes, actually you are, Ron. Remember, my rules, my game. But I'll tell you what I'm going to do, since you're one of my favorite contestants. If you answer all of the remaining questions correctly, we'll award you the grand prize, which is a shorter, condensed version of the Wrath-of-Dad Package."

"Is there a consolation prize?" he asked.

"Yes, Ron, but it involves ants and honey and a week in the backyard under a hot sun. I doubt you'd be interested."

"All righty then," Ron said, a phrase he used frequently back then, "let's get this over with."

"OK, back to the game. As I was saying, Ron, we have reason to believe the authenticity of this document—primarily because we were there. In fact, every one of us was there except you. You stayed with your grandparents that day and, if memory serves me, spent the majority of your time messing up your diapers. Your sister served as the principal in the event, which is why her name appears on the birth certificate. I remember your mother quite vividly, as she spent six hours stretched out on a table, screaming in pain, making funny faces, and calling me names. I just tried to stay out of reach and emptied the bedpan when called on. Again, Ron, I'll ask you to trust me on this. I don't forget bedpans."

"That's enough, Dad. I did it." I was getting good at this.

"You did what, Ron?"

"I made a fake adoption certificate on the computer and put Melissa's name on it."

"And then?" He was doing so well, I thought I'd let him run with it.

"And then I put it in the box with all the important papers and asked Melissa to show me her Social Security card. I put it right on top, so I knew she would find it."

"Ding—Ding—Ding! Good answer. Good answer! That concludes today's game. The sponsors wish to thank our contestants and the studio audience and invite you all back next time for 'Who Really Blew It This Time?' You can head to your room, Ron. You've got three days in the *hole*" (my term for grounded).

"Three days! But I confessed! Dad, that's not—"

"Four? Did I hear four?"

"Three days, all righty then." Ron rushed off into his bedroom with the speed and grace of a cheetah.

"As for you, young lady," I turned to Melissa, "you need to think things through before you get all upset. At the very least, come talk to Mom or me before you let something like this bother you."

"It looked real," she said.

"Yes, Sweetheart, it looks pretty real," I held up the adoption certificate for her examination, "but if you read the signature here, it says: Ima Knutt. I don't think anyone who works for the state has a name like Ima Knutt. And speaking of the state, how many are there?"

"Fifty," she answered correctly.

"That's right, fifty," I said. "Read what it says on this seal."

"State of Con . . . Confusion," Melissa read.

"Right, State of Confusion. I don't think that's one of the fifty."

Melissa laughed, Sue laughed, and I laughed; I think I even heard Ron laughing from behind his bedroom door. Sound travels in a house; I keep trying to remember that.

So if your parenting techniques don't measure up to Dr. Spock, don't let it worry you. Mine probably don't measure up to Mr. Spock either. Regardless, I think discipline was meant to make the offender aware of his or her mistakes and provide motivation for improving future behavior.

Sometimes—not all the time—we manage to do that without yelling and screaming and swatting a rear end. Nowadays their rear ends are too big to swat anyway, so we're forced to improvise.

Personally, I believe that any reasonable method when applied with consistency usually proves effective. I just hope we don't run out of game shows before our kids leave home.

"Come on, Dad! Not Jeopardy."

"Yes, Jeopardy, Melissa."

"But I don't like that game."

"Too bad. My house, my rules. Now, under the category of 'Words' for five hundred dollars: This four-letter word means to arrive home past the appointed hour. Da dum dum dum—da dum dum, da da dum dum dumm—da dum dum dum dum . . ." (I really enjoy the sound effects).

"What is 'late'?" Melissa answered.

"Correct," I said. "Remember that tomorrow when you're asked to come home an hour earlier."

"But, Dad!"

"Two hours?"

"OK, an hour. You know, your games really stink, Dad."

"You just have to learn how to play them, Sweetheart."

My son, do not despise the LORD's discipline and do not resent his

rebuke, because the LORD disciplines those he loves, as a father the son

he delights in.

Proverbs 3:11–12

CHAPTER 3

If You Could Read My Mind

I've heard it said that after many years of marriage, spouses begin to acquire certain traits from their partners. They assume the same body language, share many of the same colloquialisms in their speech, and even begin to resemble each other in attitude and appearance. Sue always gets very emotional when we discuss this subject. So deep is her love for me that the conversation often reduces her to tears, and she spends the following weeks buying new outfits and experimenting with hairstyles. Try as she might, I don't think they make her look at all like me.

What I have noticed, though, is that while she may not be able to match my receding hairline or the soft, subtle curves of my expanding waist, she has developed a knack for following my train of thought. It is a short and slow-moving train, to be sure; a coal-burning engine in this day of electric rails, but follow it she does. Sometimes I wonder if she is not the engineer, and I'm just a passenger relaxing in the safety of my own private caboose.

Why, just the other day, while I was sitting in my favorite chair watching the Knicks battle the Lakers in double overtime, my sweet, Amazing Karnack of a wife stared right through my eyes and read the very thoughts from my brain before I even realized they were there.

"I bet you were just getting ready to go outside and weed those flower beds you've been promising to take care of for the last six weeks," she said.

"Is that what I was thinking?" I asked, one eye on the television and the other straining to make contact with hers. "I felt a thought developing deep down in there somewhere, but the word *pretzel* was loosely tied to it. Oh well, I guess it's gone now."

"Just as well," Sue said, "you finished the pretzels late in the third quarter."

"Really," I said. "Tell me something, Sweetheart. Was I thinking about weeding the flower beds right this minute during the most exciting game of the year, or did I plan to wait until after the postgame interviews and the highlight clips?"

"Let me see," Sue said, and she looked deep and thoughtfully into my eyes. "As best I can tell, you were hoping to pull weeds right after the buzzer sounded and to skip all that senseless banter about a game you watched in its entirety."

"You know something, Sue? I think you're right. It's becoming very clear to me now. Boy, it sure is a good thing I have you, or I might have sat in this chair and wasted an entire afternoon."

"I'm here to help," Sue said.

Frankly, I don't know how I ever got along without her. I can't begin to list the number of times Sue has been able to read my mind and dredge up a thought that has saved me from wasting a potentially productive day engaged in some needless and idle pursuit like a sporting event or a nap on the couch. It amazes me that I accomplished anything during the years prior to our marriage.

Without Sue's uncanny ability to tell me what's on my mind, the garbage cans might never reach the street, the dog could die of starvation, and the lawn would resemble the jungle ride at any of a dozen theme parks. I'd miss every turn on every freeway and forget my own mother's birthday.

"Were you thinking of sending your mother a card?" she asks. Well, as a matter of fact I was.

"Were you thinking of taking Highway 152 so we could stop at that fruit place?" Never can have enough dried apricots, I always say.

This woman is a blessing to me; there are no two ways about it. Yet, somehow I have failed to reciprocate in like fashion. Certainly, I have assumed some of her mannerisms. The way I answer the telephone or fold a shirt can be easily traced to her. But when it comes to reading her mind, I don't know where to start.

Sue's mind is like a Tolstoy novel—beautiful and well constructed. She has an incredible depth of character, a thoroughly imaginative plot, combined with a strong and consistent theme. And as with Tolstoy's *War and Peace*, I can't seem to muddle my way through the first chapter. Not for lack of trying, no sir; I have read and reread the opening lines, pondered over the cover for hours on end. Too many twists and turns—try as I might, something always gets lost in the translation.

"Surprise, Sweetheart!" I said one evening. "I picked up four tickets to the monster truck rally at the arena."

"Why?" she asked.

"Because I thought you liked monster trucks."

"Not even a little bit," she said. "What gave you that idea?"

"You said something about it the other night when I was reading the paper."

"What I said was, 'The kids were acting like monsters on the way home from the grocery store, and we almost got side-swiped by a truck.'"

"Are you sure?" I asked. She provided a convincing argument, following which we were both absolutely sure.

I don't know why I find it so difficult to follow my wife's thought patterns, but at least I'm in pretty good company. Other men I know suffer from the same shortcoming. We even discussed it one evening during our weekly discipleship meeting.

"I know exactly what you mean," Jerry said. "It's eerie. Like some sort of *Twilight Zone* thing. Kathy always knows what I'm thinking before I do. Hours before, sometimes even days."

"Have you ever tried to read her mind?" I asked.

"I tried quite a few times in the early years of our marriage," Jerry said. "I'd sit there and stare at her until my eyes crossed, but the only thing I came away with was a headache."

"I think it's one of those things you shouldn't even mess around with," Steve said. "There's a lot of potential for trouble when you start poking into things we're not meant to understand."

"Like what?" I asked.

"Like, suppose you got lucky and actually figured out

what she was thinking," Steve said. "Then what happens? You've shown you have the ability to read her mind, and the next time you do something dumb and insensitive, your best defense is reduced to nothing more than another lame excuse."

"I don't follow you," I said.

"You've heard the statement 'Ignorance is bliss,'" Steve said.

"Yeah."

"Well, stay happy."

Being the sensitive, caring man of the nineties that I am, I was not the least bit discouraged by the cynical comments of my peers. I left the group with my determination intact, even more intent than before on uncovering the key to Sue's mind. When I got home, we started with the experiments.

"OK, Sweetheart," I said, "just sit right there."

"What do I have to do?" she asked.

"Nothing. Just sit there and look pretty while I attempt to read your mind." Her bout of uncontrolled hysterics nearly destroyed my concentration.

"I mean it," I said. "You sit there, while I try to tell you what you're thinking."

"Maybe you should start smaller," Sue suggested, "and work your way up. For example, instead of trying to read my mind, try telling me what I said to you this morning."

"When this morning?" I asked.

"Anytime before noon."

"I don't want to," I said.

"You don't *want* to," Sue asked, "or you can't?"

"OK, I don't want to because I can't. How's that, Miss Smarty Pants?"

"Well, it's honest, anyway," Sue said. "Listen, this is silly. You're never going to read my mind."

"Sounds to me like you're a little afraid I might succeed," I said.

"I'm afraid you might hurt yourself."

Not one to bow to the admonishment of my critics, I charged ahead with the experiment. "Just sit quietly and let me give this a shot," I said.

Looking deep into the sky-blue eyes of the woman I've loved for more than seventeen years, I saw the history of our lives together. In the space of a moment, I pictured the smile that greets me each morning and the friendship I've shared every day. Somewhere back behind her pupils I envisioned every joyous occasion we ever shared. The birth of our children, our first home together, even Scrabble on the living room floor came to life in my lovely wife's eyes.

"I've got it," I said. "I know what you're thinking."

"What?" she asked.

"Sex. You're thinking about sex."

"Remarkable," Sue said. "You're absolutely remarkable!"

"So I'm right?"

"Not even close! You're supposed to read *my* mind," she said, "not your own."

"OK, then. Pizza! You're thinking about pizza."

"Are you crazy?" Sue asked.

"No, but you know how sex makes me hungry."

"Well, I think we've explored that territory enough for one day," Sue said. "Kreskin will sleep tonight—secure in his job security."

"Come on, wait a minute," I pleaded. "Give me one more try."

"This is ridiculous," Sue said as she got up from the couch to leave.

"No, wait!" I said. "I've got it this time. I know what you're thinking. Give me one more chance!"

"One more," Sue said, "and then I'm going to bed."

"OK," I said. "I'm sure now. You were thinking how nice it would be if we took Friday off and drove out to that bed-and-breakfast on the coast. You were thinking about how much we'd enjoy having dinner at our favorite restaurant on the boardwalk and taking a stroll on the beach under the moonlight. How's that?"

"Perfect," Sue said. "You read my mind."

I couldn't help but think that my friend Steve was right. There are a few things men shouldn't fool with. Sometimes it is easier to remain ignorant. It is certainly cheaper, anyway.

Houses and wealth are inherited from parents, but a prudent wife

is from the LORD.

Proverbs 19:14

CHAPTER 4

Deck the Halls with Poison Ivy

"Jingle bells —
   Batman smells —
      Robin laid an . . ."

"Whoa, whoa, whoa!" I yelled, interrupting the impromptu songfest taking place on our living room floor. "What's gotten into you guys?" I addressed my children with the stern parental look I had practiced in order to communicate such moments of dissatisfaction.

"What?" Ron asked, oblivious as to the nature of their infraction. Two years his sister's senior, at age eight, Ron had already assumed his role as the pair's self-appointed spokesman.

"What?" I mimicked, "You're off key, that's what. Now try

it again, this time in the key of C . . . or B . . . or something sharp or flat. Never mind, just listen. It goes like this":

"Jingle bells—

Batman smells . . ."

My wife, Susan, a wonderful woman with an unfortunate knack for bad timing, chose this moment to walk in the front door. Unaware of my penchant for music and my gift of near-perfect pitch, she appeared surprised—dare I say awestruck—and remained motionless, mouth agape, taking in the spectacle before her.

"*You're* teaching them those songs?" Sue has never been a music aficionado and displays a total lack of appreciation for the classics.

"I don't suppose you'd believe me if I said they were teaching me?" I asked.

"Nope."

"Just as well. I couldn't say that anyway," I said. "It was purely a philosophical question. But I do want to go on record as saying your suspicious nature and accusatory tone pain me deeply."

"So noted," Sue said.

The children, having inherited bad timing from their mother, saw the following lull in our conversation as an appropriate opening for their melodic rendition of "Randolph the Red-Faced Cowboy."

"You're killing me here, you know that?" I said, glaring at my young prodigies, to which little Benedict Arnold and his sister Mata Hari responded by rolling on the floor and giggling gleefully in the face of their father's plight.

"And what other songs has Daddy taught you?" Sue asked.

"I really doubt you'd be interested," I interrupted. I had

guessed wrong, and Sue insisted on hearing their entire repertoire.

They were a fountain of information, my two little turncoats, and they spewed forth a virtual stream of familiar, if not traditional, holiday titles. I spent the next few minutes explaining that "Grandma Got Run Over by a Reindeer" was in no way directed toward my in-laws, and that, yes, I loved her mother and wished her no harm—be it at the hands (or hooves) of fawn or foe. Sue wasn't really angry, just stunned, a state of mind that has become the hallmark of our life together.

"Can't you teach them something a bit more constructive?" Sue asked, once the kids had scampered off to seek other entertainment.

"I suppose I could try," I said, "but it goes against my better nature. I'm Dad, remember? I get to play the role of the overgrown, happy-go-lucky playmate, the fun guy."

"And what does that make me?" Sue asked.

"Uh-uh, nope—not even gonna answer that one," I said, shaking my head from side to side. "You know it's unfair to ask questions that don't have correct answers." Sue laughed and threw a handful of clean laundry in my direction that had been sitting on the couch, waiting for the folding fairy to make an appearance. Normally, I would make a few sock balls and return her fire, but my present standing considered, I opted to fold and sort, a visible, if silent, demonstration of my repentance.

"You know," Sue said, folding an undershirt into thirds, "a group from the church is going caroling next week. If you want, you could teach the kids a few songs they could really use."

"Caroling?" I asked.

"Yes, caroling," she said. "What's wrong with that?"

"Look outside, Dorothy," I said, "we're not in Kansas any-more." Sue and I, both cold-climate natives, had moved to California a number of years earlier.

"What does that have to do with anything?" she asked.

"It has everything to do with it," I said. "You can't go around spreading Yuletide joy in shorts and a T-shirt. For crying out loud! You put a few cups of hot wassail in those kids, and they'll be passing out with heat stroke."

"Where is it written that you can't sing Christmas songs unless it's twenty degrees outside?" Sue asked.

"I think it's a union thing," I said. "Anyway, it just wouldn't be the same."

Despite my logical and well-presented arguments to the contrary, Sue remained intent on joining the carolers, and I reluctantly took on the responsibility of teaching the kids a few traditional Christmas tunes. We started off with "Silent Night, Holy Night," moved into "The Little Drummer Boy" and, by the end of day four, wrapped up with a favorite of mine: "Away in a Manger." In the process, I learned that young children possess an incredible capacity for memorization and absolutely no concept of melody or rhythm. Thankfully, kids are cute enough to get credit for the presentation without being judged for musical quality. I considered the endeavor a complete success.

So confident was I, in fact, that I called the kids into the kitchen and invited Sue to enjoy a special sneak preview of the Darbee Family Carolers. Pulling a pair of chairs off to one side of the room, we cleared a space in the center and sat back to enjoy the show: Sue as a spectator, me as the proud and satisfied father/coach.

"What should we sing first?" Melissa asked, anxious to display her newfound talents.

"Anything you want, Sweetheart," Sue said.

"Just pick your favorite," I added. "Show Mommy how much you've learned." I leaned back in my chair, arms folded, nose slightly tilted in the air, sporting the look of a man who has performed admirably, and achieved a measure of greatness—in short, a man ready for a major fall.

"Jingle bells—

  Batman smells—

    Robin laid an . . ."

"Now wait just a minute!" I yelled. "That's not what we've been practicing." Not to be deterred by the reaction of one dissatisfied fan, however, Ron and Melissa continued through to the end of the song's chorus.

"Don't be upset with them," Sue said, applauding Melissa's curtsy and Ron's bow. "It was a special request."

"You?" I questioned. "*You* put them up to this?"

"Sure," Sue said. "Why not? You don't have to be Dad to be the fun guy, you know. Moms can be playful too. Let me see," she continued, "if I'm the fun one, that would make you . . ."

"The other fun one," I said. "Merry Christmas, Sue."

"Merry Christmas, Sweetheart."

Sing for joy, O heavens, for the LORD has done this; shout aloud, O earth beneath. Burst into song, you mountains, you forests and all your trees, for the LORD has redeemed Jacob, he displays his glory in Israel.

Isaiah 44:23

CHAPTER 5

There's a Party Goin' On!

"Oh, come on, Mom," I mumbled, buried deep beneath my pillow and a pile of bed covers, "just ten more minutes." My previous evening's activities (*carousing*, as my mother called it) had drained me of my precious reserves, and I wanted nothing more than to sleep the morning away.

"The service begins in one hour," she answered, showing no intention to yield. "Now get your lazy behind up this instant." In what might be considered abusive by today's more "enlightened" standards, she tore the insulating layer of blankets away from my body, cruelly exposing my fragile teenage frame to the cold morning air.

"Mom!" I yelled, more an accusation than a title. I groped around the foot of my bed, eyes still closed, in search of my former warmth and security.

"I expect to see you at the breakfast table, teeth brushed and presentable, in five minutes," my mother warned, "or else I'll be back with a pitcher of ice water." Mom obviously missed the episode where Mrs. Cleaver coaxes the reluctant Beaver from his bed with the smell of smoked bacon and a stack of buttermilk pancakes.

"Dad!" I pleaded, seeking sympathy in another court.

"You heard your mother," my father answered from in front of the bathroom mirror. "Get a move on it." A man of few words, Dad never was much for the whole sympathy thing.

I went to church that morning, but I went none too happy. And in a manner consistent with teenage dissatisfaction, I made my feelings known throughout the entire service. I grumbled about my parents' choice of pews, complained about the temperature of the sanctuary, and, for the grand finale, picked apart the sermon during our short trip home.

That afternoon, sitting on the asphalt pavement, back against the pharmacy's east wall, I continued to vent my frustrations, this time to the always-open ears of my friends. "I don't know why we have to go to church, anyway," I said, not really sincere in the assertion, but throwing it out as a topic for discussion.

"Me neither," several guys chanted in agreement.

"We never go to church," Theo said, standing to bounce his rubber ball against the cement wall. "My father says if he ever went through the doors, the building would collapse around our feet, and he'd be responsible for the needless deaths of hundreds."

Surprised by the chorus of support my earlier grumbling had obtained and possibly feeling a tinge of guilt, I sought to clarify my position, so as not to appear a complete pagan in the eyes of my friends or, for that matter, anyone else who might be watching. "I don't really mind going to church," I said, "I just think I'm old enough to have a choice."

"You guys are crazy," Anthony Gianelli said, trying to gain control of the conversation. As the group's self-proclaimed leader, control was something Tony always sought to obtain. "You gotta go to church. That's the rule."

"Whose rule?" someone asked.

"God's rule, that's who," Tony delivered his response with a certain finality, as if his answer was so clear, the meaning so obvious, that only a complete moron would require any form of elaboration. With little to lose in the way of intellectual standing, and more than a few painful memories attributed to Tony's unique doctrinal interpretations, I decided to seek clarification.

"Where exactly did this rule come from?" I asked.

"From the Bible, Nimrod," Tony answered. "Don't you know anything? Look, it's like this: You gotta go to church if you wanna go to heaven. I don't think I can make it any easier for you. You can miss a week here and there," Tony continued, "maybe even two, if you're sick and can't get out of bed. But start missin' three or four times in a row, and you'll spend eternity wearin' asbestos underwear and beggin' for a glass of ice water." Tony's unique theological observations were based on truths gleaned from many hours of DC comics and the occasional catechism class. Unusual as it was for the group to disregard Tony's scholarly observations, we chose to continue our conversation in spite of the benefit his wisdom provided.

"My mom says she goes to church to see what everyone else is wearing," Andy said. "That and if we don't go, people will start talking about us." Several other reasons surfaced, everything from: "My dad is a deacon and it wouldn't look right if we didn't go," to "My mother says I'm gonna be a priest someday, so I might as well get used to it."

Micky, the smallest and, by survival instinct, quietest member of our group, saw the time as right to add his own two cents to our conversation, no doubt doubling its accumulated value. "I like to go to church," Micky said.

Several shouts and jeers followed his comment, but also one request for the squirt to expand on his previous statement. Whether he was coaxed out of sincere curiosity or targeted for further abuse, I'll never know. Whatever the case, Micky continued to share his opinions.

"It's like God is throwin' a big party every Sunday," Micky said, "and it wouldn't be right not to show up. Besides," he continued, "I've got a lot to be thankful for, and that's just my way of lettin' him know it."

The rest of the conversation escapes me. Though I stayed through its conclusion, I failed to hear anything else that was said. From my frame of reference, Micky had the least to be thankful for. Abandoned by his parents—the details of which I never knew—he was shifted between a variety of aunts and uncles over the years before finding a permanent home with his grandmother. She couldn't give him very much, but apparently she gave him what she had—a strong faith and a very thankful heart. I felt more than a little guilty for my own lack of gratitude and my actions earlier in the day.

I suppose we all lose perspective from time to time, get caught up in the workings of church, and forget to take part in the celebration. If we're not careful, church becomes something that happens around us, rather than something we cause to happen. Micky understood that worship is a celebration and an expression of thanks. I appreciate the example he left in my memories.

Did I rise early the next Sunday, with shouts of joy and songs of praise the moment my mother came to wake me? Not on your life! I begged and pleaded for a few more minutes of sleep; such is the way of teenagers. But I did go with a different outlook, a changed perspective.

These days, I'm the first one up on Sunday morning; I have my own pair of teenagers to rouse.

"Hey, lazybones, get up. You'll miss the party."

"Oh, come on, Dad. Just ten more minutes."

"I'm going to get the ice water," I threaten. OK, so I'm not exactly Ward Cleaver. But who is, anyway?

Yet a time is coming and has now come when the true worshipers will worship the Father in spirit and truth, for they are the kind of worshipers the Father seeks.

John 4:23

CHAPTER 6

A Man's Home
Is His Hassle

OK, so I don't know the difference between a joist and a jamb. I couldn't point out a plenum if it were the only thing in the room, and furring strips sound like they belong in a taxidermist's office. The only frost line I know anything about is in our freezer; coping is how I make it through the day; and no one will ever convince me that flashing has any place on my roof. What kind of neighborhood is this, anyway?

I should have ignored that guidance counselor in high school, along with his misguided advice. While all my friends went to shop class to make sheet metal ashtrays for non-smoking parents, I wasted away in geometry worrying about the area of a triangle. While they built cutting boards in wood shop and tore apart engines in automotive, I learned how to find the cosine of an angle. Anyone ask you for the cosine of an angle lately? Me neither, but I bet you own a cutting board or two—maybe even three.

Being the product of an education burdened with academics, I am mechanically inept, assembly disadvantaged, and renovation impaired. In my hands, a two-dollar repair job becomes a two-hundred-dollar bid for replacement; an oil leak transforms into an engine overhaul, and leaky faucets bloom into decorative fountains. When I fix something, I fix it but good, and teams of skilled craftsmen spend days, sometimes weeks, completely engrossed in the process of unfixing it.

I have come to believe that "Some adult assembly required" refers to somebody else, and "Build it at home" doesn't include mine. Unfortunately, *believing* and *accepting* are two entirely different concepts. I have long ago embraced the former and live my life in complete denial of the latter. It's not my fault, I reason. Most assembly instructions are written by English-as-a-seventh-language students, and the diagrams look like something we hung on the refrigerator when Melissa attended kindergarten. License plates may be manufactured in prisons, but do-it-yourself kits are obviously packaged by mental patients in our country's darkest asylums.

Why then, knowing my limitations, with evidence of my failures piled throughout our garage, do I insist on playing handyman around the house? Because even in a society that claims to turn a blind eye to sexual stereotypes, men are expected to know a crescent wrench from a crescent roll. We are allowed one vice, but only if it is spelled with an *s* and attached to the corner of a workbench. In short, I suffer from pride and refuse to admit my failure to live up to an expected standard.

Sue, on the other hand, is not burdened with pride and

finds little problem admitting my failure or reminding me of it as new projects take shape. I call it *criticism,* but she sees it as nothing more than protecting our investment.

"Where are you going with that toolbox?" Sue asked as I attempted to sneak through the living room en route to a leaky faucet. "Nowhere," I said, and tried to hide the tools behind my back.

"If you're not going anywhere, what do you plan to do with that toolbox?" she asked.

"Nothing."

"Pardon me for saying so," Sue said, "but I don't believe you."

"Once again, your lack of trust brings me great pain," I said. Not one who easily succumbs to false guilt, Sue stuck to the line of questioning. "You weren't thinking of messing around with that faucet, were you?"

"Come on, Sweetheart," I said. "All it takes is the right tool for the right job, and considering all the stuff I crammed into this box, the right tool must be in here somewhere."

"The right tool is hanging on the wall in the kitchen," Sue said. "It's called a *telephone.* Please call someone who knows what they're doing."

"I know what I'm doing!"

"I love you," Sue said, "and I respect your abilities. But history suggests you do not know what you're doing when it comes to home repairs."

"Those were all practice runs," I said. "I learned from my mistakes, and now I'm going to capitalize from the experience gained."

"So far, your plumbing experience hasn't produced much gain," Sue said. "You turned our toilet into a power-scrub bidet, took the life out of our Shower Massage, and collapsed the bathtub fixture with a pair of channel locks."

"Like I'm supposed to know how soft brass is?" I defended.

"No, you're not supposed to know how soft brass is," Sue said, "and that's why you call someone who does. Now will you please call a plumber?"

"Fine," I said. "We'll call a plumber, but I'm not dialing the number. If you want a plumber, you'll have to call him yourself." The only thing I intended to call was Sue's bluff, so confident was I that she would never go through with it.

The guy pulled up in front of our house within the hour. A real smug, know-it-all kind of handyman, with his fancy tools and, from the view I caught as he checked below our sink, an apparent aversion to suspenders or a belt.

Now, if there is one thing I absolutely despise—even more than calling a professional to rescue me from a bind—it is deceptive advertising. Claims like: Earn fifty thousand a year in only three hours a week. Lose inches from your waist in four days and eat everything you want. Vote for me and we'll build a bridge into the twenty-first century. Ads like that make people distrustful, even cynical, about what they read, see, and hear through the media.

But if anything bothers me more than deceptive advertising, it is truthful advertising that hits a little too close to home. The side of this guy's van boasted the following claim: "We fix what your husband fixed first." Now that simply is not called for.

The guy was friendly enough, in a huffy, know-it-all kind of way; he went right to work on the problem, acting as if he knew just from looking at it what needed to be done. Sue seemed mildly impressed with his craftsmanship, but he didn't fool me for a minute. It was a lucky shot in the dark that he grabbed the right tool on the first time out.

"Careful with that," I advised after he removed the handle

and grabbed hold of the fixture with his plier-looking thing. "That's brass, you know. Really soft metal."

"Thanks," he said. "I'll be careful."

"Probably collapsed a few of those in your day, I'd imagine," I said, and looked to Sue with a knowing glance.

"Nope."

"Come on," I said. "Not even once?"

"Nope."

Like I said, a real know-it-all kind of guy. "Well, did you ever tie a supply line into the drain by mistake and send water shooting up through every sink in the house?" I gave Sue another knowing glance.

"What?" he asked. He looked at me like I just made the top ten idiots list and was making a run for number one.

"Well, you know how easy it is to make a mistake," I said. "You get down there under the house, and—what with all the spiders and the darkness and everything—one pipe looks pretty much like the next. I'm sure you've screwed up your fair share of projects."

"Mister," my plumber friend said, "how do you make your living?"

"Me? Well, I work with electronics, high-voltage mostly—a laser development project at the Livermore laboratory."

"And I take it you know what you're doing?" he asked.

"For the most part," I said. "Though I think you could get an argument if you looked hard enough."

"And this laser thing," the plumber said, "probably took some time to learn, required a little education, maybe?"

"Well, yeah, of course," I said. "You don't start playing around with eighty thousand volts of electricity until you know what you're doing."

"You probably wouldn't hire me for that job, would you?"

he asked. I hemmed and hawed a bit, feeling somewhat uncomfortable being put on the spot like that.

"Not a problem," the plumber said. "I don't have the skills to do your job any more than you have the skills to do mine. So I ask you, what's the difference between you and me?"

"Not much, I guess," I said, "except I don't make ninety dollars an hour."

"You don't work up to your elbows in someone else's toilet, either," he said.

"Good point," I said. "You just might be underpaid."

"Remember that when you see the bill."

"Listen," I said, "do you mind slowing down a bit, so I can learn something while you're fixing this?"

"I've got all the time in the world, mister. It's your nickel."

Actually, it was more like my hundred-and-forty bucks, but I view it as money well spent.

Whether we're men or women, pride sometimes gets the best of us. The world makes it easy to believe that we are less than adequate in one area or another—sometimes we feel that we should be better than we are. A climate is created in which it is difficult to admit what we don't know, and pride invites us to pretend.

At the risk of furthering a stereotype, I think men struggle with this issue more than women, though we certainly don't have a corner on the market. I know I hate to see a need in my home or family that I can't fulfill. I want to be the fix-it guy, whether that means repairing a leaky faucet, speeding up a fastball, or mending a broken relationship.

I am a husband, and I am a father. I have a number of perceptions as to the responsibilities those titles hold. But I do so appreciate the occasional reminder that God doesn't expect me to be everything to everybody all of the time. He has gifted each of us with certain talents, guiding us in particular directions. He doesn't require me to be the best plumber, only the best me that through him I can become.

"Have you been in the bathroom recently?" Sue asked as I surfed the channels with my remote.

"That depends," I said. "Did I leave a towel on the floor, or something?"

"No, it's that faucet," she said. "It's leaking again, and it's only been a week."

"Yessssss!" I shouted, and performed the modified/stationary version of my happy dance.

"Should we call a different plumber," Sue asked, "or try to get the same guy out here again?"

"No, get the same guy. I'm sure he'll stand behind his work, Sweetheart," I said. "Let's give him another shot. Besides, there's something about that guy I liked. Call it personality or charisma. I just have a good feeling about him."

If the whole body were an eye, where would the sense of hearing be?

If the whole body were an ear, where would the sense of smell be? But in

fact God has arranged the parts in the body, every one of them, just as

he wanted them to be.

1 Corinthians 12:17–18

CHAPTER 1

Heaven — You've Seen the Ads, Now Read the Preview

There are no brussels sprouts in heaven. In fact, heaven may be completely devoid of vegetables . . . with the possible exception of corn, and then only the cobbed variety, certainly nothing canned or creamed.

I developed this obviously deep theological philosophy over the dinner hour sometime during my eighth year. Staring down the business end of my mother's wooden spoon, the unhappy recipient of a barrage of threats designed to accelerate my digestive process, I began to form a few opinions concerning the perfect world, and more to the point, a perfect eternal world. No, brussels sprouts wouldn't appear on the menu, of that I was certain. But what would heaven hold for an eight-year-old boy?

My parents would be there, no question, though on somewhat more equal footing. With angels to pick up my room and handle the monotony of my chores, Mom, Dad, and I could settle into a relationship as peers. No more fussing and arguing about taking out the garbage or cleaning up my mess—let Gabriel handle the small stuff.

As for my older brother, Jimmy, he'd probably squeak in under the gate, but God would have a few words to say to him regarding his outrageous behavior and the continual mistreatment of his innocent younger brother. True perfection would find Jimmy a couple inches shorter than me and destined to wear my hand-me-down robes for the next couple of millennia. After all, God is just, right?

Heaven lends itself easily to speculation. My own childish consideration of the subject stretched well beyond the dinner table and into the streets and playgrounds of New York. Waiting to choose sides for stickball or walking home from school, it wasn't unusual to ponder the question of life after death. We were for it, heavily in favor of an eternal utopian existence, though in no particular hurry to speed the process along.

I'm willing to guess we've all thought about heaven now and then: what it must be like, where it's located, if reservations are recommended—maybe even required. According to a recent Gallup poll, 90 percent of us believe in heaven, although only 73 percent believe in hell. I don't know if that means Americans as a whole are optimistic or just plain scared, but it's interesting, all the same. It's got me to wonderin' what some of our cultural icons might think about heaven—Bart Simpson and Wile E. Coyote, Arnold Schwarzenegger and Bill Clinton (paired for contrast, not comparison).

While barbecuing at a friend's house recently, I passed

out a number of index cards, each carrying the name of a famous or infamous person or character. Everyone was asked to consider the public life and examples of their assignment and write a paragraph describing how that person might perceive heaven. Following is a sort of "What-if" speculation, some best guesses as to how we thought some folk in the spotlight might see heaven.

Bart Simpson— Sometimes described as the attitude with a bad haircut, Bart probably sees heaven as the ultimate toy store complete with a satellite dish (imagine the reception) and multi-function remote control. If there's a blackboard anywhere to be found, you can bet Bart anticipates an eternity of writing repetitive phrases like: I will not pull the wings off angels; martyr jokes are not funny; and I will not try to erase names from the Book of Life.

Arnold Schwarzenegger— You've heard of *Conan the Barbarian*; one or two people actually saw *Conan the Destroyer*, but is *Conan the Saint* within the realm of possibilities? In heaven, Arnold would hope for an unlimited supply of the best Cuban cigars (apparently smoking hasn't stunted the big fella's growth), movie reviews that described him as an eloquent orator, and a heartfelt conversion of his in-laws (the Kennedy family) to the Republican Party. If his tombstone reads "I'll be back," don't count on it.

Clint Eastwood —

Clint has witnessed a great deal during his tenure in Hollywood. He's seen the good, the bad, and the ugly sides of life. Chances are the pale rider would just as soon ride off into the sunset on a slow horse and contemplate the theme of his most successful movie: *Unforgiven*.

Any Congressman —

Don't allow this category to confuse you. We are not here to debate whether politicians *can* go to heaven, just what they think it would be like. Certainly they would see heaven as the ultimate one-party system, although some might be uncomfortable with the idea of God holding full veto power. Considering the recent failures to impose term limits, I'm sure most fully grasp the concept of an eternal resting place.

F. Lee Bailey— Possibly our country's best-known lawyer, I believe Mr. Bailey might question the age-old adage, "You can't take it with you." Recent circumstances regarding his refusal to hand over mandated assets to the court indicates a willingness to go the distance in attempting to hold onto what he believes is his. However, he may see heaven as a great storehouse of treasure and be willing to give it a fair trial. With God as the ultimate judge, Mr. Bailey may harbor a few fears about getting his objections pushed through.

Wile E. Coyote— The Acme Corporation does not have a distributorship in heaven, at least not as far as Wile E. is concerned. I have it on good authority that Mr. Coyote believes heaven is populated with an abundance of extremely slow road runners, all completely ignorant of his brilliance as a hunter and tactician.

Cal Ripken— When Cal Ripken broke Lou Gehrig's record for most consecutive games played, he won a place in the hearts of many

Bill Gates —

baseball fans. Here is another man who can understand eternity, which is slightly longer than he's been playing baseball. The CEO of Microsoft Corporation probably considers heaven the last untouched market. With new operating systems and software upgrades coming at the pace of one per year, a guy can peddle a lot of CD-ROMs over the course of eternity. Bill would like to wait a while before passing through the pearly gates, however. He knows all about demo versions and bug reports, and wants to be sure everything is worked out ahead of time.

Dr. Kevorkian —

I have no idea if Doctor Kevorkian believes in heaven, but you can be sure the man is betting his life against the existence of hell.

Well, it can be fun to speculate on how others might possibly view heaven, but eventually we are faced with determining for ourselves what we really believe. My views have certainly changed since I was eight years old. I still want to see my parents there, and I stand firm on the whole brussels sprouts concept, but I've expanded my base of knowledge somewhat.

Jesus described heaven as a place of joy, celebration, and fellowship with the one true God. He spoke of heaven in terms of hope and glory. He even mentioned treasures, an inheritance that can't be stolen or lost. And wouldn't you know it? He gave a complete and simple set of directions. "I am the way and the truth and the life," Christ said (John 14:6).

I've got to tell you, I made my reservations, and they're even guaranteed. Try getting that from Club Med.

"And if I go and prepare a place for you, I will come back and take you to be with me that you also may be where I am. You know the way to the place where I am going." Thomas said to him, "Lord, we don't know where you are going, so how can we know the way?" Jesus answered, "I am the way and the truth and the life. No one comes to the Father except through me."

John 14:3–6

CHAPTER 8

Teenagers — A Study in Linguistics

I was not eavesdropping, just sitting in the next room attempting to concentrate, when the conversation overflowed and interrupted my solitude. It's not as if I actually understood the dialect they were speaking, anyway. They are teenagers, after all, and I am just an oldie. I returned my attention to the work at hand, but every time a thought developed, my daughter and her friend took their conversation up a notch, challenging me, or so it seemed, to involve myself in their affairs.

"What do you think of (insert some acne-faced boy's name here)?" my daughter said.

"Ohhhhh, he's the bomb!" her friend screamed.

That's it; I've had enough, I thought. *I'll just ask them politely to keep the noise down while I'm working. They'll understand.* I got up from the table and walked down the hall to Melissa's bedroom door. Two teenage girls giggled in response to my knock.

"Sorry, Dad," Melissa said, opening her bedroom door. "Are we making too much noise?"

"Afraid so, Sweetheart. Listen, I'm sorry to ask, but could you guys keep it down until I finish working? You can march a six-piece band through here when I'm done, but right now I need some peace and quiet."

"OK, sorry."

"Sorry, Mr. Darbee," her friend echoed the apology.

"No problem," I said. "By the way, what's a bomb?"

"Da-a-a-a-a-d!" Melissa screamed. "You were listening to our conversation."

"Melissa, I couldn't help but listen to your conversation. I really wasn't trying, but sound carries through the vents, you know."

"Yeah, right," was her embarrassed reply.

"So tell me, anyway," I continued, "what's a bomb?"

"Da-a-a-a-d," Melissa repeated in disgust.

"It's '*the* bomb,' Mr. Darbee," her friend said, "not '*a* bomb.' He's the bomb means, like, he's the daddy."

"The daddy of what?" I said, violating my own request for quiet conversation.

"Not the daddy of anything," she said, "just the daddy. Like, the coolest guy around or something."

"Well, if you don't mind, I'd like to think of myself as the only daddy around here for a while," I said. "And by the way, is it 'bomb' like in an explosion, or 'balm' like a salve or cream?"

"Da-a-a-a-d!" Melissa yelled for the third time, and it was obvious I had overstayed my welcome — assuming I was welcome in the first place.

"Sorry, girls," I said. "I was just trying to understand the vernacular."

"Ver . . . what?" Melissa's friend asked.

"Vernacular," I said; "it refers to the spoken language of a culture as opposed to the literary language."

"Dumb word," Melissa said.

"Yeah, well, I'll leave you girls alone now,"

As my kids get older, I'm finding it more difficult to effectively communicate with them in terms we both understand. Granted, our parents faced much the same issue, but it couldn't have been this difficult. Sure, we added a few new words to the dictionary (*groovy* died a merciful death, although *cool* still makes the rounds), but this generation has turned everything completely around.

For example, when Michael Jackson sang, "I'm bad," I agreed with him wholeheartedly. I'd go so far as to say he was horrible, but as it turns out, bad meant good, so *horrible* is likely the ultimate of compliments—not the message I wanted to convey. Nowadays, "That's stupid" is a positive endorsement, and calling a friend "dope" doesn't even elicit an argument.

My kids have removed the word *said* from their vocabulary almost completely, replacing it with the modern synonym *all*. Take this excerpt from one of Melissa's phone calls, for instance:

"And like, my dad's all, 'No, you can't go to the movies tonight.' And I'm all, 'But, Dad, please.' And he's all, 'No, you've got school tomorrow.' And I'm all, 'So!'"

There is a lull in the conversation at this point, while (I assume) her friend on the other end of the line punches all of this into her secret decoder ring and forms an equally unintelligible response.

"No, I can't," Melissa continued, "He's in dictator mode or something. He's all, 'No, and that's final,' and he'll like go postal if I ask again."

Following that conversation, I didn't know if I should be angry or hire a speech therapist and lexicographer to bring her up to speed.

It almost seemed easier to understand the kids when they were toddlers, just a year or two old. I listen to a friend's child now, and at a year-and-a-half his seventeen-word vocabulary proves adequate for all of his needs. Stephen Michael Ruble's (using his full name is not an obvious ploy to sell extra copies of this book to his grandparents) entire lexicon consists of nine nouns (mommy, daddy, sister, cat, dog, duck, pooh — as in Winnie — bath, and ball), three adverbs (yes, no, and please), and three adjectives (hot, cold, and bad.) A pair of pronouns round out his vocabulary. He is a young man of few words, to be sure, but he says what he means and means what he says. I find him to be a skilled and effective communicator, and I enjoy our many in-depth conversations.

My own son, Ron, on the other hand, possesses a much broader vocabulary, and it is getting broader all the time. While I believe that he intends to say what he means, his success rate falls shy of 100 percent.

"Dad, you're not going to believe this," Ron said.

"What am I not going to believe?" I asked.

"You know how Cory and his parents are always arguing," Ron asked, "and how he ran away from home a couple of times, got in trouble with the police, and went to live with his aunt once?"

"Yeah, I think I've heard something along those lines," I answered.

"Well, he decided he wanted to make his own decisions;

the court said it was OK, so he asked his parents, and they eviscerated him."

"They what?" I asked.

"They eviscerated him," Ron said. "I'm serious."

"Are you sure, Ron," I asked. "I mean, it seems a little harsh to me."

"Positive. I talked to Josh, and he said they eviscerated him yesterday; now he can make his own decisions."

"Yeah," I said, "but for how long?"

"Huh?"

"Ron, *eviscerated* means disemboweled. I don't think that's the word you're looking for."

"Emaciated?" Ron asked.

"Nope, still too strict even if he were having some problems with the law. I think you mean emancipated, Ron."

"Oh yeah. That's it," Ron said. "Hey, I think it would be pretty cool to make my own decisions, Dad. What are the chances of you emancipating me?"

"Zero," I said. "As a matter of fact, your mother and I were talking about asking for an extension that covers you beyond your eighteenth birthday."

"Yeah, right, Dad."

"But hey," I said, "if you want to be eviscerated, we can talk about that for a while."

So communicating with teenagers can be difficult. At least we're talking, and I figure we're getting a little better at it with every new attempt. I'm starting to pick up on the colloquialisms and the slang, and they're trying to be patient with me as I learn. Given enough time, I'm sure we'll understand each other completely.

"What do you think of this shirt, Melissa?" I asked, fixing my tie in the mirror.

"It's bad, Dad," Melissa said.

"Thank you, Sweetheart."

"No, I mean it's really bad," Melissa said.

"Well, that's nice of you to say. Your mother picked it out for me."

"Dad, it's horrible," she yelled. "It's the ugliest shirt I've ever seen!"

"Oh, cut it out, Melissa. All these compliments are going to go to my head."

So it is with you. Unless you speak intelligible words with your tongue, how will anyone know what you are saying? You will just be speaking into the air. Undoubtedly there are all sorts of languages in the world, yet none of them is without meaning. If then I do not grasp the meaning of what someone is saying, I am a foreigner to the speaker, and he is a foreigner to me.

1 Corinthians 14:9–11

CHAPTER 9

A Guy's Guide to Gift-Giving

Through arduous research and keen, detailed observation, I have stumbled across a truth of such magnitude, a fact so important, I would consider myself remiss if I failed to share it with friends and readers. Here goes:

Men and women are different.

I realize my findings may set the entire psycho-babble industry on its ear, but that is a risk one must take when arduous research and keen, detailed observation come to fruition and reveal a truth so simple and pure. Worry not, for I have no intention of resting on the laurels of this great discovery and fully intend to continue unearthing other truths, both arduously and keenly.

Perhaps when I release my findings in more scholarly

form, I will make reference to the obvious physical and emotional differences between the sexes. I'll mention the differing needs and expectations, allude to the contrasting hopes for career and family, and touch on concepts like *communication* and *intimacy*. But the substantiating point, the true foundation of my thesis, will be built upon the subtle yet obvious divergence of attitudes when it comes to the subject of gift-giving. So few have labored in this important field, I find myself a pioneer of sorts, forging a new trail for my brothers to follow, a rugged passage between the florist and Macy's.

Among the weighty questions men have posed throughout history — Who do you like in the Superbowl? What is the big deal about the toilet seat? Who asked you, anyway? — there lies one, as of yet, unanswered mystery: What do I buy my wife, girlfriend, or mother that will convey the proper message for any one of a number of holidays? I believe my study holds the answer, and I share my efforts with you now in a demonstration of brotherhood and solidarity.

First, we must establish and agree on one basic truth that serves as the cornerstone for this theory: Women view gift-giving as an opportunity; men see it as an obligation.

Case in point: In the course of shopping, women frequently come across an item that reminds them of a friend or triggers a pleasant memory. They often purchase said trinket, wrap it up, and present it as a symbol of friendship. There are no strings attached, no special occasion to celebrate. It is simply an opportunity to brighten someone's day, a chance to express love and caring, or to identify a special relationship.

"I saw this at Mervyn's and knew it would look great on you," a woman says to her daughter-in-law, handing her a beautifully wrapped package containing a sweater, three pairs of slacks, coordinating socks, earrings, and one of those elastic things women wear in their hair. "I found these gorgeous little duck-shaped soaps at the flea market," another woman says, "and immediately thought of your bathroom. I hope you like them." She hands the soap to her friend, who, of course, absolutely loves them, not because she perceives a shortage of ducks adorning her bath, but because they represent the well-meaning intentions of someone who cares about her.

Men, of course, never do this. No, some men charge into department stores, grab a clerk by the shoulders and shake briskly, screaming: "It's my wife's birthday today! What have you got?" The clerk, properly trained in the art of antagonizing distraught husbands, responds: "Well I don't know, sir. What does she like?" The husband, already late getting home from work and realizing he doesn't have the time to inflict a level of pain the turncoat so obviously deserves, yells back: "If I knew that, I wouldn't need you!" The diabolical clerk then suggests a bottle of perfume, slightly more expensive per ounce than gold. Confused, and in panic, the husband releases the clerk, grabs the first kitchen gadget he sees, and pays cash so the credit card bill doesn't reveal the last-minute nature of his purchase. It happens every day.

Occasionally a man, looking for a quick and easy solution to the problem of finding an appropriate gift for the woman in his life, mistakenly enlists the aid of one of her friends as a sort of shopping consultant. While this philosophy appears to have merit on the surface, it is dangerous ground and should be crossed lightly. In fact, I recommend avoiding this method completely.

Let us take, for example, the case of a young man who enlists his girlfriend's best friend to aid him in the effort of purchasing a special occasion gift. If memory serves me, that might be something like a six-and-one-half month anniversary of the first time they ate chicken together at Colonel Sanders's place. (It is not at all unlikely that they will have separate anniversaries for regular and extra-crispy.) Assuming the poor lout remembers this momentous day (which he won't), he will need a gift suitable for the occasion. I believe plastic is recommended in most of the etiquette books, but clothing or jewelry is always an acceptable alternative.

Thanks to the assistance provided by his sweetheart's friend, our hero arrives bearing gift. We'll choose clothing for this example. The young lady is overjoyed that her beau remembered the day, opens the package, and is pleasantly surprised—dare I say awestruck—by the appropriateness of his gift. It is her exact size and favorite color. It is consistent with her sense of style. It matches several items already part of her wardrobe. Houston, we have a problem.

The young lady is certain to draw one of three conclusions at this point, all of them bad.

1. Her boyfriend had a great deal of help in purchasing the gift, in which case he loses all points accrued for thoughtfulness and good taste.

2. Somewhere along the line, the young gentleman has gained considerable experience in buying women's clothing, which—unless he has several sisters—brings up questions about past relationships he would prefer to leave unanswered.

3. The boyfriend is actually an observant, caring young man who possesses a level of sensitivity not often displayed by the gender. Chuckle, chuckle. Try to keep that facade standing for any length of time.

Mothers, on the other hand, give little reason for concern. By the time we reach the age of gift-giving accountability, our fathers have paved the way, already desensitizing them to most of our masculine shortcomings. In other words, their expectations aren't very high. How difficult is it to please the woman who made such a fuss over the plaster of paris hand imprint you brought home in kindergarten? If Moms can celebrate our first successful attempts at combing our hair, laud us for riding bicycles without training wheels, and consider us "above average" regardless of what our test scores indicate, they aren't very difficult to please. Buy her something nice, and she'll stick it on the mantel with a dozen other baubles she has collected over the years.

With the preliminaries out of the way, it's time to get down to business and develop a gift-giving strategy. We wouldn't leave the huddle without calling a play; likewise, men should never conduct a relationship without forming a gift-giving strategy. We'll use a typical married man for this example.

First, consider keeping a spare present on hand for emergency occasions. Jewelry serves well as an all-purpose gift, and is easily hidden in the sock drawer for retrieval at a moment's notice. It is extremely important to label the gift, however. I cannot overstress the seriousness of this point. Should your wife stumble across a pair of earrings in your sock drawer three months before her birthday, displaying her name in clear and bold print will benefit all involved.

Second, when buying clothes, exercise extreme caution regarding size. Women's clothing does not follow the same reasonable labeling standards men are familiar with.

As a newlywed, I once attempted to buy an outfit for my wife, and assuming her waist was somewhere around twenty-eight inches, asked the salesperson for a size 28. Not yet trained in the art of antagonizing distraught male consumers, the clerk kindly pointed out that women's sizes are labeled differently: 6, 8, 10, 12, and so on. While a larger size does correspond to overall mass, the number is otherwise meaningless,

relating in some fashion to phases of the moon, date of manu-
facture, or something along those lines. Had I actually brought
home a size 28, I would have found myself camping beneath
it in my backyard for at least a week.

Get a feel for the size your wife wears — not by asking her,
never ask, but by comparing the tags in her closet. When in
doubt, buy small. It is much easier to say, "Honey, you just
look like a 6 to me," than, "Keep the 18, Sweetheart. Maybe
you'll grow into it."

Third, avoid kitchen gadgets and appliances not specifically requested, anything involved with cleaning (unless you
buy her maid service), and items you are likely to use more
than or as much as she will.

Fourth, consider the perceived message. A trip to a health
spa is good, enrollment in Jenny Craig is bad. A candlelight
dinner at a fine restaurant wins points, an all-you-can-eat buf-
fet draws a penalty flag.

Last and most important, every gift should meet the following criteria. It should be extremely heartfelt — a gift that
says something about who she is and what she means to you.
It should be timely and thoughtful — purchased at least a day
in advance and from an establishment that doesn't pump gas.
Above all else, it should have a receipt marked, "Returns
Gladly Accepted." Past that, I'm afraid you're on your own.

Don't be deceived, my dear brothers. Every good and perfect gift is

from above, coming down from the Father of the heavenly lights, who

does not change like shifting shadows.

James 1:16–17

CHAPTER 10

Encroaching the Throne

Home! I threw the gearshift forward, set the parking brake, and removed my key from the ignition. Slowly, carefully, I turned my head to the side and surveyed the fifteen feet or so separating me from the sanctity of my front door. I could make it. Maybe not with style, and certainly a little shy of pizzazz, but with a fair amount of effort, I could pick up my briefcase and drag what remained of Ron Darbee up the sidewalk and into my quiet, peaceful home. Friday—I love Fridays.

I opened the car door and swung out first one leg, then another, and using the armrest for balance, pushed my tired frame to a modified standing position. *Forget the briefcase,* I thought. *It will be there on Monday when I start this routine all over again.*

56

I took the fifteen-foot hike in slow and methodical fashion. It felt as if I carried the entire defensive line of the New York Giants on my shoulders. The old Giants, back when Lawrence Taylor ate quarterbacks for breakfast and all was well in football. But I knew I would cross the goal line. I had vision. I had purpose. My chair awaited me.

Our home is full of chairs: desk chairs, kitchen chairs, chairs in the bedroom and in the garage, chairs that rock and chairs that recline, wooden chairs, beanbag chairs, highchairs, and folding chairs. If there's a chair for the job, we probably own a set. But there is only one chair I call my own.

Like my father before me and his father before him, I have a designated retreat positioned strategically in front of the television. It is the Remote Control Command Center, recliner extraordinaire, a haven for the weary father, my own private, personal throne. It is where I make decisions and take naps. It is the seat from which I read *The Little Engine That Could* to my children and explained the birds-and-the-bees. Report cards come directly to this chair, as do letters addressed, "To the Parents of . . ." and problems that require Dad's attention.

I know my chair, and it knows me. Every broken spring holds a story. Every creak and groan of the mechanism sounds like music to my ears. It no longer looks like it did in the showroom, but I don't mind because it belongs to me. Of that there has been no question—at least not until recently.

I made it to the door that Friday, into the entryway, and through the kitchen. It was when I turned the corner that I noticed something was amiss. I saw a pair of sneakers through the doorway, two feet off the ground and where my own belonged. They were the shoes of a usurper, a pretender to the throne.

"Comfortable?" I asked the reclining shape that belonged to my son.

"Yup."

"Can I get you anything? Maybe a soda or some pretzels? I think there are cookies in the cupboard."

"Nope, I'm fine," he answered. "But it's really nice of you to ask." His sister sat on the couch across the room, surveying the situation and taking a few mental notes.

"Well," I continued, "I think a young man should be as comfortable as possible during his last few moments on earth."

"Do you mean me?" he asked. "I'm not going anywhere." He wore a smile—half grin, half smirk—and it was obvious he intended to put up a fight.

"Move it or lose it," I said in that Robert Young, *Father Knows Best,* sort of way.

"Nope."

"OK," I said, "last chance. Get thy mangy backside out of my chair, Goatboy, or suffer your father's wrath."

"O-o-o-h-h-h-h, I'm really scared."

I could see this tack wasn't working and settled on another course. "Come on, Ron, please," I pleaded. "Your Dad is really tired. All I want to do is sit down for a while and relax."

"Plenty of room over there on the nice, comfortable couch," he said, pointing in the direction of his sister. "Feel free to take all the room you want." Melissa, sensing her time had come to join in the festivities, spread herself flat, taking up as much room as her thirteen-year-old body could manage.

"I'm sitting here," she announced with a giggle.

"OK," I said, "I didn't want to do this, but you forced me.

Sue!" I yelled, calling to their mother for assistance. "Your kids won't let me have my chair."

"Poor baby," she said, mock sympathy in her voice, and turning to the children, "Let your poor old daddy have his chair, before he starts to cry."

"Who said anything about crying?" I questioned. "I only solicited your help to save our children from the pain and embarrassment of their father demonstrating his physical superiority. Actually," I continued, "I planned to throw Goatboy for distance and was concerned his Royal Girthness might land on Melissa, crushing her and rendering her incapable of performing household chores."

"Are those tears I see forming?" Sue asked, now solidifying her position in the enemy camp. A chorus of "Daddy's crying, Daddy's crying" rose up from my offspring, and I realized that somewhere along the way I had lost control.

"All right. All right, fine," I said. "Have a little fun at my expense. I'll go in the backyard and lie in my hammock."

"Oh, let your father have his chair, Ron," Sue said to our son. "They don't have much time left together. I suppose we ought to let him say good-bye."

"Good-bye?" I queried. "What's this about good-bye?"

"The income tax refund came in today's mail," Sue said. "We agreed we'd buy new furniture for the living room."

"The chair's not furniture," I said. "It's . . . it's *my* chair!"

"You act like it's one of the children," Sue said.

"Not at all. That chair never talks back to me. The chair's loyal and comfortable and dependable."

"D-a-a-a-a-a-d!" Melissa yelled.

"Quiet, Sweetheart. Your mother and I are talking."

"We agreed," Sue reminded me.

"Not really," I countered. "You were unclear when we discussed this. You didn't specifically mention my recliner. I agreed under false pretenses—under duress. That's it; I agreed under duress. Your argument will never hold up in court."

"Are you through yet?"

"That depends, do you still plan on replacing my chair?"

"It's old and worn out," Sue argued. "The entire right side leans out at an angle. How many times have you lost the remote down there?"

"And is that my fate, as well?" I asked. "When I'm old and worn out, when I lean to one side, then will you get rid of me too?"

"You're still here, aren't you?"

"OK, then, Sue. If my chair goes, so does the coffee table and both end tables. How do you like those apples?"

"It's a deal. I'll call Good Will tomorrow."

Sometimes I fear I'm not the sharpest pencil in the box. This feeling usually overcomes me shortly after I open my mouth.

We browsed through nearly every furniture store in the northern San Joaquin valley the next day, and while Sue found tables, a couch, and several other items she was perfectly happy with, I didn't see one suitable chair. Some were too big, others too small. A scarce few of the chairs reclined to the optimum angle, and none felt as comfortable as my personal throne. Several even boasted a few hi-tech extras like adjustable lumbar, built-in cup holders, and holsters for multiple remote controls. Let them keep their vibrating massage and heat control. I wanted my chair.

The drive home could have been more pleasant. Sue called me "picky" and accused me of intentionally finding fault with every La-Z-Boy® that came my way. Of course, I told her she was being ridiculous, but it didn't help. It looked as if we were in for a cold and quiet evening. But then I got an idea.

I pulled the car to the side of the road and began presenting my idea, first in the form of a question. "What's the first rule for a happy marriage?" I asked.

"What are you talking about?"

"Come on, the first rule. What is it?"

"Don't leave your dirty underwear on the floor by the bed?" Sue guessed.

"No, come on. I'm serious."

"This isn't going to be an 'honor your husband' lecture is it?" Sue asked.

"Nothing like that," I said. "*Compromise* is the answer. Marriage requires compromise."

"And what's your idea of compromise? Do we keep all of the old furniture?"

"No," I said, "we reupholster the chair. You can pick the fabric to match the new couch, I'll have all the springs resprung and the side bolted back into place. My chair will look like new and, best of all, it will still be my chair. Come on, Sweetheart, what do you think?"

"It might work," she said. "We can have it restuffed and reshaped." She paused for a moment to ponder the perceived pluses and minuses of the situation. "Mr. Darbee, you've got yourself a deal." She offered her hand to seal our agreement.

"Thank you, Mrs. Darbee. It's been a pleasure doing business with you."

My chair and I are very happy. It maintains the favored spot in front of our television and remains the Remote Control Command Center, a place from which I can still dispense wisdom. I didn't have the heart to show Sue the bill from the upholstery shop. We could have bought two chairs for the price, but compromise is healthy for a marriage—everybody wins and nobody loses. Who knows, we may have opportunity to try it again sometime.

"Honey, I'm home!" I yelled, slamming the front door behind me. I set my briefcase down and made a beeline for the living room. Once again, I saw feet breaking the plane of the doorway.

"Move it or lose it, Goat—" I cut myself off in mid sentence. "Sue, why are you in my chair?"

"*Our* chair," she said.

I think I see another compromise on the horizon.

Settle matters quickly with your adversary who is taking you to court. Do it while you are still with him on the way, or he may hand you over to the judge, and the judge may hand you over to the officer, and you may be thrown into prison.

Matthew 5:25

CHAPTER 11

Road Warriors

So you're driving down the highway in the left lane, occasionally passing a car to your right, when you get the indication that someone behind you is dissatisfied with your rate of speed and would welcome an opportunity to pass. The gentleman to your rear, the typical shy and reserved type, indicates his desire by subtly flashing his high beams, applying the entirety of his considerable weight to the horn, and edging his vehicle close enough to your rear as to qualify for passenger status.

Sure, you're a wee bit annoyed, possibly even slightly aggravated, but the obviously Christian thing to do is to immediately begin praying for the distraught soul following you. In the spirit of brotherly love and concern, you slam on your brakes, intending to commence your prayerful petition right that very moment. Your new friend, seeing his entire life flash before him in the form of your taillights and not interested in ending his days as an adornment to your rear bumper, swerves to the left—his wish granted—as he shoots past you at a high rate of speed, quite a feat really, considering two of his wheels are in the roadside ditch.

Now you're a bright person. You suddenly realize how this deed of Christian kindness might be misconstrued as a malicious and spiteful act of retribution, so you put the prayerful petition on hold for a more appropriate time, resume your forward momentum, and continue along your merry way. A few hundred yards down the road, you pass the harried driver who, just moments ago, seemed in such a hurry. It appears his driving habits have undergone a sudden change.

For one, your friend is now in the right lane. His speed appears somewhat shy of thirty miles per hour, and his hands are in the ten- and two-o'clock positions. He seems to be sweating, shaking, and coughing up something that resembles—yes—it's his tongue. You wave as a demonstration of concern and caring for this obviously troubled man.

Oh, look! He's a mime! Well trained in the art of hand gestures, the driver puts on an impromptu roadside show, demonstrating for you—his only audience—a unique set of skills meant to both communicate and entertain.

An exaggeration? Maybe not.

In 1988 I gave up my amateur status, set aside my college eligibility, and received full certification. I joined the ranks of the professional commuter, defined as anyone who drives more than thirty miles in one direction at least four days a week (fifteen miles if you're unfortunate enough to pilot a passenger vehicle in a major city, bonus points if the city happens to be New York or Los Angeles).

In a way, I looked forward to the added quiet time, a chance to unwind and think things through at the end of a hectic day. I anticipated a calm and peaceful jaunt from my home to the office, followed by a restful and relaxing return trip. What I failed to anticipate was the million or so drivers accompanying me on the road to Shangri-la, some slightly agitated, others downright angry. Their attitudes were horrible, their driving skills menacing, and I found the entire package quite contagious.

They're just a little stressed out, I thought after a few weeks of watching my fellow commuters swerve in and out of lanes like hamsters racing for cheese in a maze. That guy driving on the shoulder probably has a medical emergency. That's it, he's a doctor! Shy of transporting a vital organ to some sick child prepped for surgery, I couldn't think of any reason for pushing sixty on loose gravel. The other drivers lacked my insight and keen reasoning skills, however, and displayed their dissatisfaction in individual, and often inappropriate, ways.

By the three-month mark, my good nature started to wane. Even considering the number of vital organs in the human body, there just can't be that many liver, heart, and lung transplants. Some of these maniacs, certainly not all, had less than legitimate reasons for their behavior. I began to suspect, and I was almost ashamed to admit it, their actions represented nothing more than a desire to get home quickly. Please forgive my cynical nature.

When the calendar marked my one-year anniversary on the road, I was completely acclimated. Gone were any misconceptions about the motives of my fellow commuters. They were animals, each and every one, and the only rule of the road was every man for himself. These weren't mere commuters. They were athletes participating in the most dangerous full-contact sport since the Romans trained gladiators—

parolees from some prison for homicidal demolition drivers. But by now, I fit in.

Demonstrations of anger and violent behavior are becoming more prevalent on our nation's highways. As more vehicles crowd the roadways, more interactions occur between drivers, supposed affronts increase, and tempers begin to rise. For most, the problem ends there—a little aggravation and nothing more. But an increasing number of drivers are responding in aggressive and dangerous ways. Experts call it "Road Rage," and it in some way affects every person on the road, either as participant or potential victim.

Perhaps most disturbing to me is the ease with which I found myself moving closer to participant and farther from the ranks of spectator. When you are alone in a car, surrounded by three thousand pounds of metal and viewing the world through a tinted windshield, it is easy to feel separated from other drivers. There is a false sense of privacy, even seclusion, in an automobile. When tempers begin to rise we direct aggression at not another person but another vehicle, an inanimate object that has in some way caused offense. It sounds silly to a reasonable, thinking human being. But I promise you, there are few people reasoning or thinking during stop-and-go rush hour commutes.

Two things happened to make me reevaluate my driving attitude and institute some changes. First, a woman in our small group politely asked if I would consider removing the fish placard from the rear of my truck. She pointed out that my driving habits might offend those not familiar with my good nature and made a convincing argument regarding the advertisement of Christianity and the violation of traffic laws. That hurt, but the second incident held the potential for greater pain.

I was driving down the road, on my way to pick up lunch and in a hurry to get back to work. Stuck in the slow-moving right lane, I began to grow agitated with the inconsiderate bozo meandering along at twenty-five miles per hour in front of me. Traffic to my left was preceding at a much more desirable pace, but I couldn't find an opening to move into that lane. My temperature started to rise — I didn't want to be late getting back to work. My blood began to boil. Who was this tourist taking in the sights and keeping me from my goal? I decided to help him along a bit.

Moving my high-riding, four-wheel-drive utility vehicle as close to the bumper of his sports car as possible, I hoped to transmit my desire for speed via the picture of my grill in his rearview mirror. Subtle, I know, and he didn't pick up on the hint. I leaned on the horn, hoping to state in clearer fashion my urge to speed up the pace. Nothing. The headlights flashing didn't make my point either, and I began to get very aggravated.

Finally, after what seemed like a week, but probably wasn't more than a few minutes, I found an opening to my left and accelerated into the fast lane. It was important to me at that time to express my dissatisfaction with the Mustang's driver, and as I passed, I looked directly into his tinted window, scowled my fiercest scowl, and waved a sarcastic thumbs up. "Nice driving, Buddy!" I yelled through the open passenger window. The man rolled down his window and waved. He appeared to be amused. He appeared to be my employer.

When I arrived back at work — and you can bet I arrived on time — I made it a point to stop by his office and offer my apology. "Hey," I said, "Have you ever been driving down the road, become real aggravated, and made a fool of yourself in front of your boss?"

"Nope. How does that feel?"

"Bad," I said. "Really bad."

"I bet." At least he was smiling. I took that as a good sign.

"You're getting a real kick out of this, aren't you?" I asked.

"Yup."

"OK, well, I'll be going now. Just thought I'd drop by and apologize." I'm glad he took it so well. It could have been much worse.

I'm a much better driver now, and I am conscious of how my actions behind the wheel make a statement about who I am and what I believe. I even share my commute with a friend these days.

"Did you see that guy blow by us on the shoulder?" my rider asked one morning.

"Yeah, I know him," I said. "He's a doctor, I think. Delivers organ transplants for sick kids or something."

"But he's driving a pickup truck. There are ladders and paint cans and drop cloths in the back."

"He doesn't like to look too conspicuous," I said. "Just trust me on this one, please. It's easier in the long run. Believe me, it's easier."

You are all sons of the light and sons of the day. We do not belong

to the night or to the darkness. So then, let us not be like others, who are

asleep, but let us be alert and self-controlled.

1 Thessalonians 5:5–6

CHAPTER 12

Confessions of a Nursery Attendant

The placard to my left read, "Sleepers and Creepers." "Crawlers and Fallers" adorned the door on my right, and I could see "Walkers and Squawkers" a little farther down the hallway.

"Nice signs," I said to Craig, our Children's Ministries pastor. "They sound like they belong on the primate exhibit at the San Diego Zoo. You picked them out yourself, I presume?"

"Keep laughing, smart guy," Craig said. "We'll see how your sense of humor is holding up at the end of the month."

"Cake walk," I returned, confidence evident in my voice. "No problem. Four weeks working in the nursery will seem like a vacation compared to setting up the sanctuary for morning services. I'll read a few stories, play a couple of games, and fill the little tykes up with cookies and milk while their parents worship in confidence. I ask you, could this get any easier?"

"You really should consider counseling," Craig answered. "You've reached a stage of delusion that requires a professional's touch."

Maybe an explanation is in order. Craig and I have built a friendship over the last six or seven years, and like many male friendships, ours includes a fair amount of well-intentioned ribbing, the verbal equivalent of a friendly punch in the arm. We often go back and forth in a good-natured manner, kidding each other about some topic of the moment, like his receding hairline or my expanding waistline. Of course, as with all forms of conversation, the risk exists of placing one's foot firmly and decisively in one's own mouth; that is what led to my introduction to the nursery that morning.

I guess a guy can only take a few hundred cracks about having it easy in the children's wing or growing up and becoming a "big people's" pastor before he starts to take it personally and draws a line in the sand. Apparently, I had exceeded the magic number because Craig challenged me to experience for myself the vacation I perceived as his life. Not being bright enough to back down, I accepted his challenge and agreed to work a month in the nursery. Thankfully, the month contained only four Sundays.

So that I don't sound like a complete ogre, let me say that I do honestly love children. I have learned, however, that I love them much more in groups numbering less than thirty, with increasing affection as the total falls below five. Two is absolutely perfect, and if those two happen to be mine, so much the better.

Following Craig's brief introductory tour of the facilities, I joined the harried ranks of the nursery attendants. I do confess that my perceptions of children's ministry have undergone some serious revision. It seems that our smallest members possess an incredible insight on the emotional and spiritual aspects of life. Allow me to share with you a few simple truths I learned from our children.

Personal Contentment Is a Matter of Perspective:

- A clean diaper, a dry nose, and a warm bottle of milk solve most of life's little problems.

- You can put a square peg into a round hole if you hammer at it long enough.

- It is fun to put together puzzles, even if they are all missing one critical piece.

There Is a Greater Power:

- You're never too young to pray, but you can be old enough to forget how important it really is.

- It is OK to ask for help, especially if you don't know how to work the zipper.

- I am loved. I was put here for a reason, and someone is coming back for me soon.

How I Treat Others Affects How They Will Treat Me:

- If I take someone else's toy, someone will take it from me.

- Sharing improves everybody's attitude.

- Yelling doesn't make anything clearer, only louder.

Goals Are Good. Good Goals Are Better:

- Stuffing the most M&Ms in your nose doesn't necessarily make you the winner.

- Learning to walk is a great accomplishment, but sometimes it is nice to be carried.

- I'm going to get bigger whether I worry about it or not.

Diet Is a Popular Topic of Discussion:

- Candy tastes better than paste. Paste tastes better than crayons, and crayons make your teeth turn funny colors.

- Just because one cookie is good, and two cookies are better, doesn't mean that twelve cookies is the best of ideas.

- Everything tastes better if you like the person who gave it to you.

Is there more to children's ministries than I realized? Absolutely! Just between us, I might even have stayed a few extra weeks if they'd have let me. I learned too much to leave after only four weeks. There is something about working with children—showing them they are loved and cared for, modeling the Word of God, and teaching them when the opportunity presents itself—that refreshes those truths in ourselves. As for my relationship with Pastor Craig, I don't think it's likely to change very much.

"So, Ron," Craig asked following my four-week tour in the children's wing, "you look like you've put on a few pounds. Dipped into my snack cupboard in the nursery, did you?" "Maybe a little," I answered. "By the way, when do you plan on giving up the baby-sitting routine and looking for a real job?"

Our wives gave us each a "time-out" until we learn to play nice together. I think it might be a while.

People were also bringing babies to Jesus to have him touch them.

When the disciples saw this, they rebuked them. But Jesus called the

children to him and said, "Let the little children come to me, and do not

hinder them, for the kingdom of God belongs to such as these."

Luke 18:15–16

CHAPTER 13

My Life's Application

"Can too!"

"Can not!"

"Can too!!"

"Can not!!"

"Can too!!!" I said it with conviction this last time to let Sue know I meant business.

"I don't care what the guys in your discipleship group told you. We're entering the twenty-first century, and you can't arrange your daughter's marriage." Sue acted like some sort of expert on the subject, and I was supposed to respect her opinion like the law itself.

"Show me where it's written," I said. "Give me documented evidence and I'll shut up."

"I don't know why I even discuss these things with you," Sue complained. "I let you drag me into these ridiculous conversations about something that isn't even going to happen for at least another seven years —"

"Twelve," I corrected.

"You see! There you go again. Melissa is only thirteen years old, and you want to argue about when she's going to get married."

"Who's arguing?" I asked. "I'm not arguing. I'm stating a point of fact: twenty-five and not a day sooner. And I still say if we raise her with certain expectations, she'll be perfectly willing to let us arrange the marriage for her — somebody from a good Christian family. Trust me on this."

"I could have you committed on this," Sue said. She tends to get irrational when an argument doesn't go her way.

Speaking as a man raised without the benefit of sisters, I find fathering a daughter one of the most challenging and absolutely terrifying experiences God ever sent my way. While my son lends his own brand of anxiety to our already anxious lives, it pales in comparison to the pure, unadulterated fear with which I view raising a young lady. Boys, I understand. I used to be one. I know how they think and what they want from life. And it is because I know what makes these little testosterone-fueled clocks tick that I don't want my daughter giving any of them the time of day.

Don't get me wrong, I love Melissa immensely and never considered trading her for a son. The bond between father and daughter is unique and incredible, a relationship filled with its own special rewards and unlike any I've ever known. But it is also a relationship that strikes terror into the hearts of fathers the world over as our sweet, darling princesses blossom into womanhood. We begin to view neighborhood boys, not as the sprouting young leaders of tomorrow, but as predatory adolescent hunters, preying on our precious offspring. Take my word for it, I know.

I never really understood my father-in-law until I had a daughter of my own. That cleared up a lot of my perceptions, and I came to a gradual understanding regarding how Sue's father initially felt about me.

I was an eighteen-year-old private first class, a few months out of Marine boot camp when I flew to Minnesota to meet Sue's family. Sue and I met the weekend I graduated from Parris Island, and I was about to marry the first woman I saw — literally. Not that I planned it that way, it just happened to work out. We dated for a few months and decided to make a lifelong commitment as husband and wife. Our trip to Minnesota was scheduled to inform Sue's parents of our plans and invite them to share in our happiness.

Normally you would expect, as I certainly did, a guy would be overjoyed with the prospect of his daughter making such a fine match. I was employed, after all, pulling down a huge income as one of Uncle Sam's finest. I had youth, good health, and a sharp uniform in my favor, and every intention of passing my driver's test the next time around. Could a father really want anything more for his daughter? The signals I received suggested he wanted considerably more, up to and possibly including my head on a silver platter.

The father of my betrothed didn't view our courtship with the same enthusiasm Sue and I shared. What we considered a Cinderella-story-turned-whirlwind-romance, he saw as two eighteen-year-old children about to embark on the most devastating mistake of their lives. To his credit, he remained polite and distantly cordial during the entirety of our visit, but in a terse, I-want-you-dead sort of way. I now understand—completely.

If my eighteen-year-old daughter waltzed into our home and announced her plans to marry a young Marine, I'm not sure I would handle it with the same grace and noticeable absence of violent threats. I'd like to think I would prayerfully petition my heavenly Father, something out of Job or Lamentations, probably, and ask for his guidance on the young couple. I'd like even more to think it will never happen at all.

That's why I've developed an application—nothing fancy, just a short, six-page form designed to screen out undesirable suitors and identify prospective candidates for courtship. This way my princess need not worry herself with the dull and dreary business of finding a young man she likes. Dad will take care of everything.

Application to Date My Daughter

Welcome, prospective suitor, to the qualifying phase of the date-selection process. Let me be the first to congratulate you on passing the preliminary screening sections of our qualifications. Please bear in mind that your acceptance into this stage of the process is based on a local police records check, and your application cannot be considered final until the results of the name, fingerprint, and retina scan information now under investigation by the FBI is received and reviewed to my satisfaction. Similarly, while drug screening samples submitted to our laboratories are clean, weekly samples will be required should you advance to the courting phase.

Last Name: _____ First Name: _____
Middle Initial: ___
    Aliases, Nicknames, or Family Names: _____
_____

Note 1: If you listed: Stud, Lover Boy, Lady Killer, or anything of a similar nature, place your pencil on the table in front of you and proceed quickly to the nearest exit. Stopping to discuss this issue with the proctor is not recommended.

Date of Birth: _____
Date of Baptism: _____
Date of Last Communion:_____
Social Security #: _____ Student ID #: ___
Drivers License #: ___
Grade Point Average: _____ PSAT Score: _____
SAT Score: _____
Street Address: _____
City/State: _____ Zip Code: ____
Home Phone #: _____
Cellular Phone #: _____ Pager #: _____
Next of Kin: _____ Relationship: _____
Phone #: _____
Years of perfect Sunday School Attendance:
_____

Make/Model of Vehicle (Vans, pickups w/camper shells, and station wagons strictly prohibited!):
_____

Please list any identifying marks, scars, tattoos or body piercing for the purpose of identifying your corpse should you suffer an unfortunate accident while dating my daughter (just a formality): _____

_____

_____

_____

If you listed any tattoos or body piercing, refer to Note 1 and follow the directions for exiting this facility.

What church does your father pastor or serve in the capacity of deacon or elder? _____

_____

Give a brief personal statement of faith (include major doctrinal points): _____

_____

_____

_____

List the Christian college you plan to attend and your intended major: _____

_____

Essay Portion

Choose any five of the five essay questions below and answer each in two hundred words exactly. You have thirty minutes to complete this section. Additional paper will not be provided.

1. Finish the following thought: Chastity is important to me because . . . _____

_____

_____

_____

2. Explain what rights you believe a girl's father has in disciplining her boyfriend. _____
_____
_____
_____

3. In your own words, describe the perfect chaperone. _____
_____
_____
_____

4. Describe the difference between friendship and love. _____
_____
_____
_____

5. Discuss Einstein's Theory of Relativity (provide supporting formulas). _____
_____
_____

Bible Knowledge

Answer each question below from memory:
1. The Bible is divided into how many Testaments?
_____
How many books? _____
How many words? _____
2. Moses sent twelve men to explore the land of Canaan. Name them. _____
_____

3. List the genealogy of Christ as it appears in Matthew 1:1–17 (spelling counts). _____

_____

_____

_____

4. What were the Hebrew names of Shadrach, Meshach, and Abednego? _____

_____

5. In the second year of King Darius, on the first day of the sixth month, the word of the Lord came through the prophet Haggai to whom? _____

_____

6. Provide a brief synopsis of the Book of Revelation.

_____

_____

_____

_____

Multiple Choice

Circle all that apply:

1. It is appropriate for me to touch your daughter under the following circumstances:

    A. Never

    B. Once we are married

    C. If she is on fire or about to fall off of a cliff

    D. When we have known each other for some time and are both in agreement

2. First base, second base, and third base refer to:

    A. Three corners of a baseball diamond

    B. I don't know

C. A classic Abbott and Costello routine

D. How far a girl will go

3. I like to take my dates to:

A. Church

B. "G"-rated movies

C. Wherever their fathers tell me

D. Drive-in movies or bars

4. My biggest struggles with sin are in the area(s) of:

A. Pride

B. My finances

C. Jealousy

D. Lust

5. A girl's father should be:

A. Feared, respected, feared, honored, feared, and obeyed

B. Feared, respected, honored, and obeyed

C. Respected and honored

D. Deceived

If you answered "D" to any of the questions above, refer to Note 1 and follow the directions for exiting this facility.

Thank you for participating in the application portion of our date-screening process. Your interest in our daughter is appreciated in a way you will never fully comprehend. Rest assured this application will receive the full attention of our staff, and you will be notified within two years of your grade and eligibility status. Do not call, visit, or in any way attempt to contact the party on whose behalf this application was submitted prior to receiving written confirmation of your eligibility.

—End of Application—

One day Naomi her mother-in-law said to her, "My daughter, should I not try to find a home for you, where you will be well provided for?"

Ruth 3:1

CHAPTER 14

An Exercise in Moderation

Like any other day, I went to work and performed my job in what I considered an admirable fashion. I plowed through stacks of paper, ate lunch with a friend, and mediated a personnel dispute before anyone screamed "blood feud" or threatened to pursue legal action. My boss was smiling. My coworkers were smiling. My employees didn't appear to be plotting my early demise. Overall, the day looked like an eight on a scale of one to ten—as good as anything gets between Monday and Friday.

At no time during my busy day did I intentionally cause another person harm. I didn't scare an innocent child or wreak havoc with the environment—I even swerved to avoid flattening the neighbor's cat, though I clearly owned the right-of-way. In short, my activities offered no clues as to why my evening should prove less than peaceful. I'll blame original sin, but one can never tell.

Arriving home, I brought my daughter out to the curb, played with the garbage, and asked my wife, Susan, if she had finished her homework. To be honest, I don't remember the exact order of things as my world went from serene to chaotic several moments later. I do know that I made it to the living room, where I planted myself in the soil that is my favorite chair, intent on spreading roots deep into the upholstery. Sue entered the room with a question on her mind, and that's when things got blurry.

"Do I look fat?" Sue asked. I shot a quick glance out the window, thinking I heard a fire engine go by, but I realized the sirens and bells were coming from inside of my head: a masculine warning system I had installed years earlier.

"Nope." Granted, it was a weak answer, but I needed to stall for time while I formulated a sensitive and caring response.

"I mean it, do I look fat?" Sue turned from side to side, offering me both profiles of a body I knew quite well after more than a decade of marriage. I felt comfortable, confident even, in giving an answer that was honest and uplifting.

"You look great," I said. "I love you just the way you are."

"So I am fat," she said, looking a little dejected.

In a vain attempt to diffuse the situation, I proposed a few alternate topics of conversation. "Why don't we talk about my mother or how we discipline the kids or anything else of a less controversial nature?" I asked.

"No, it's all right," she said, "I know I've put on a few extra pounds. We grew fat and lazy when we hit thirty, and now we're paying the price."

"I'm sorry?" I said, seeking clarification on a minor point. "But was that a 'we' I heard? How did this half of we—perfectly content and minding my own business, I might add—move from our living room to the lobby of Jenny Craig in the simple turn of a phrase?"

"I'm not saying this to be mean," Sue continued. "It's a fact. We've allowed ourselves to get comfortable and put on some extra weight. Now we look a little dumpy. Believe me, we're in this together."

Not yet ready to surrender Twinkies and concede defeat, I stuck with a favorite mainstay—denial—and added one last argument. "In some countries a few extra pounds is considered a sign of success." It didn't even sound good to me when I said it.

"Well, in this country, it's considered a sign of cardiac arrest." From the look of determination, I concluded Sue's mind was made up, and we were both in for a change.

I could provide a list of reasons why Sue's point hit home, not the least of which was that she was right. We had relaxed our lifestyle over the years and allowed ourselves to get out of shape. But what really gave credibility to her claims was that Sue knows what it means to be physically fit.

We met in the Marine Corps, where we both served tours on active duty. Young, healthy, and undoubtedly in the best physical condition of our lives, we gained some experience in the areas of exercise and fitness. While the training methods we endured leaned toward the harsh side, the results were inarguable. Sue played basketball on the women's regional championship team, and I ran the three-mile course in under eighteen minutes. We were in great shape.

"OK," I said, "so maybe we've let ourselves go. What do we do about it?" Had I realized the repercussions involved, I would never have asked that question.

"Let's start exercising together," Sue said. "Remember how it used to be? We'd hold each other's feet for sit-ups, pace each other on runs, and shoot baskets in the gym after work."

"It was a lot of fun," I remembered fondly. "But I'm not playing basketball with you."

"Why not?" Sue asked.

"Because you're better than me, and no guy likes to get stuffed under the basket by his wife."

"You big baby."

"True," I said, "but we're still not playing basketball. I'm in for the rest, though. It might be fun to regain a bit of our youth."

It was not our youth that we discovered over the next few weeks. Normally, Sue provides the voice of reason in our lives, while I charge blindly ahead, blissfully ignorant and consumed with some hobby or interest of the day. But she was a driven woman, intent on toning up, and *moderation* no longer found a place in her vocabulary. She was living in my world, and since I am incapable of defining *moderation,* much less encouraging reasonable behavior, we were on a course for disaster.

With no regard for rational or prudent exercise strategies, we jumped into a routine similar to the one we conducted a decade ago. We played tennis on Monday, racquetball on Tuesday, and joined a coed volleyball league that met on Wednesday nights. Thursday meant aerobics, though we both agreed to forgo Spandex for the less embarrassing look of cotton, and we set aside Fridays for whatever miscellaneous torture one or the other derived.

In a moment of concession brought on by my weakened physical condition, I agreed to play basketball on Saturdays, but that was only in our driveway during hours of minimum pedestrian traffic. I saw no sense in letting the neighbors see me huddled under the basket, my wife rising toward the rim. We jogged each morning, if you could call our pace a jog, and left Sundays as a much-needed day of rest.

On the third Sunday morning, lying in bed trying to identify the various sources of our pain, Sue rolled over and whispered something sweet in my ear.

"O-o-w-w-w-w-w," she whimpered. It was obvious that the pain had spread to her jaws and gums.

"A-a-a-h-h-h-h," I responded, and realized I must have sprained my tongue while gasping for air the previous afternoon.

"I think I decided something," Sue said. "If I want the body of a twenty-year-old, it might be easier to kidnap one and force her to come home with me."

"Forget it," I said. "It'll be months before you're in any condition to catch one."

"Do you think we overdid it a little?" Sue asked, lying still and conserving her energy.

"Could be," I said. "Tell me, is there a muscle that connects all the bones to every single nerve ending? Because if there is, I think mine's torn or broken, at the very least sprained."

"I think so," Sue answered. "Mine hurts too, but not the toes. I can't even feel my toes."

"Lucky," I said.

"What do you say we take a few days off," Sue suggested, "and reevaluate our fitness plan and goals? Maybe we could slow down a pace or two and ease into this exercise routine."

I tried to nod my agreement, but the effort shot pains through my shoulders and neck. "Yes," was my one-word response, emphatic, yet succinct.

And so ended our excursion into extreme physical fitness. We still exercise regularly—a game of tennis here and there, some two-on-two in the driveway with the kids. We walk every evening after dinner, and enjoy the occasional team sport. But the voice of moderation has returned to our household. Balance has become the new catch phrase, and we try to avoid letting any one activity consume us.

"Mom, what's Dad doing locked in the study?" I overheard the conversation in the kitchen.

"Trying to memorize the entire Gospel of John," Sue answered.

"Wouldn't it make sense to memorize a few verses at a time?" my daughter asked.

"You might think so," Sue said, and they carried their discussion into another room.

So maybe I don't learn as fast as some people. But I do eventually learn.

For it is commendable if a man bears up under the pain of unjust suffering because he is conscious of God. But how is it to your credit if you receive a beating for doing wrong and endure it? But if you suffer for doing good and you endure it, this is commendable before God.

1 Peter 2:19–20

CHAPTER 15

Driving the Lesson Home

"Get out of the car, please." I said it quietly—cautiously measuring my words so they would fit through gritted teeth.

"Dad, wait a minute. It's no big deal." Ron tried to minimize the issue, a classic teenage strategy.

"Get out of the car, now."

"Dad, come on. It was a mistake. I thought I had more room on that side. It could happen to anyone."

"Remove the key from the ignition, Ron. Open your door, and make a hasty retreat from behind that steering wheel. Do it now. Do it quickly. Do it, Son, before I do something your mother will surely regret."

"Dad, please," he pleaded.

"That's it!" I threw open the passenger's door, unbuckled the safety belt (a device I admired with a newfound high re-

gard), offered a brief prayer of thanks for the security of pas-
senger-side airbags, fifteen-mile-an-hour bumpers, crash dum-
mies, and walked briskly around the back end of the car. Ron
came out of the driver's side like a missile before I even cleared
the trunk and made directly for the passenger's door. Wisely,
the boy chose the alternate route around the front of the vehicle, and our paths never met.

"Dad, you're overreacting," Ron accused as he fumbled
with his safety belt. "It wasn't my fault. I didn't know it was
there."

"The curb? You didn't know the curb was there?" I yelled.
"It's a stationary object, Ron! It's not like a cat or a dog or a
mongoose or something. Curbs don't jump out in front of you
while you're driving down the street. And let me tell you
something else," I continued. "That lady raking her lawn knew
it was there. As a matter of fact, I bet she counted on it. I bet
she got up this morning and said to herself, 'I can go outside
and rake my lawn in perfect peace and confidence, knowing
nobody will run me over, because I have a curb and sidewalk
separating me from the lunatics driving down my street!'"

"Dad, nobody got hurt. It was just a mistake. I didn't do
it on purpose."

"O-h-h-h-h-h, well, that makes it OK, then. You didn't do
it on purpose. Let's go back and tell that nice Mrs. Johnson
she made a big deal out of nothing. 'You didn't have to dive
into your hedges, Mrs. Johnson. You were never in any real
danger. After all, he didn't do it on purpose.'"

"She seemed fine when we left, Dad."

"Really? You think?" I asked. "I don't remember seeing
her kneeling on the front lawn screaming, 'Thank you, Jesus!'
over and over again in the eight years we've lived here. Maybe
I missed that part of her daily routine."

No further conversation took place on our short ride

home. Ron was too chastised and embarrassed to speak and me angry enough to know better. Sue had no trouble determining Ron's first driving lesson went poorly by the looks we each wore. Unfortunately, his younger sister didn't inherit her mother's sense of perception.

"Was it cool, Ron?" Melissa asked, eager to hear the details and share in her brother's newly acquired feeling of independence. "Leave me alone," were Ron's only words as he stomped down the hallway and slammed the door to his room behind him.

"What happened?" Sue asked, bracing herself for the worst.

"Mario Andretti, Jr., in there tried to take the corner of First and Summit like he was racing for the checkered flag at Daytona," I explained. "He put two wheels onto the sidewalk, where I got a brief but memorable glimpse into the terror-filled eyes of Mrs. Johnson as we careened past her rhododendrons."

"Was anybody hurt? Is the car OK?"

"Everyone's fine," I answered. "We might want to have the front end realigned, but no visible damage. And as for Mrs. Johnson, she brings new meaning to the word *spry*. She leapt behind her junipers, hit the ground, and did a perfect tuck-and-roll. I'm telling you, she would have put a paratrooper to shame."

"Was she angry?" Sue asked, always interested in maintaining our relationships with the neighbors.

"No, I don't think so," I said. "Shook up a little, maybe, but praising God and shouting hallelujah for all the world to hear. She may be Presbyterian, but I think she spoke in tongues. She probably cut the battery life of her pacemaker by 50 percent too."

"I'll be sure to send her a card tomorrow," Sue said. "Now how about Ron? How's he doing?"

"Ron? He's fine," I said. "Like water off a duck's back. It's not his fault. It's no big deal. It was just a mistake. You know the routine."

"He seemed pretty upset when you guys got home. You didn't embarrass him, did you?"

"*Me* embarrass *him?* Sue, the kid was driving on the sidewalk. Life doesn't get much more embarrassing than that."

"I know," Sue said, "but he probably felt bad enough on his own. I hope you didn't make him feel any worse."

"OK, so I yelled at him. What did you want me to do, pat him on the back and hand him the safe-driving award? He could have killed somebody!"

"Maybe we should talk about this later," Sue suggested, "after you've had a chance to calm down."

After you've had a chance to calm down. I let that line settle for a moment, probably the effect Sue intended. *Maybe I was a little hard on him,* I thought. *After all, driving is a new skill for Ron. There are bound to be a few problems, a mishap here and there. Nobody's perfect. So why did I lose my temper?*

The answer to that question came easily: I was scared out of my socks. You don't have much time to think in these situations, and fear is a natural response. I was afraid for my safety and Ron's, afraid for Mrs. Johnson, and afraid of the damage my car might incur—all of this in only a matter of seconds. Granted, my reaction might have been better had Ron accepted responsibility, but he didn't have much time to think, either. We both reacted quickly and poorly, and this was a trait far more acceptable in a teenager than in his father. I knew what I had to do.

"Who is it?" Ron asked in response to the knocking at his bedroom door.

"It's me," I said. "I want to talk to you about this afternoon."

"The door's open." His invitation lacked enthusiasm, but was about what I expected considering our recent interaction. Ron was sitting on his bottom bunk reading when I entered. Back against the wall and feet up on the mattress, this is what I have come to know as his "thinking" position. He didn't bother to look up when I came in; he didn't acknowledge that I was in the room. I took a seat at the other end of the bed, back against the headboard, and thought about what I wanted to say. The words seemed so much clearer to me from out in the hallway.

"Ah, Ron," I started, "do you want to talk about what happened today?"

"Do I have a choice?"

"Not much of one," I said. "The way I see it, you can let me apologize for losing my temper and listen to my ideas for improving the situation, or you can shut me out completely, sit in here sulking until you turn eighteen, and hope your mother slips some food under your door from time to time."

"I guess I'll take the first one."

"Good choice," I said. "Your mom made soup for dinner, and it probably would have made a mess of the carpet. Look, Ron, I realize I lost my temper, and I'm sorry for that. You're at an age where you're going to try a lot of new things, and mistakes will have greater consequences. What I'm trying to say is that I'll try to show a little more patience, and I hope you'll bear with me and take your responsibilities seriously."

"Yeah, OK, Dad. I'm sorry too. I'll try to pay more attention when I'm driving. So when do I get behind the wheel again?"

"Right now, if you'd like," I told him. "We can find an empty parking lot—one without any concrete barriers, and you can practice all you want."

"Cool," he answered. "And, Dad, how did you do the first time Grandpa took you driving?"

"Not very well," I said. "We ran into a bit of a communication problem. I was driving down a two-lane, undivided highway, and your grandfather told me I should try a three-point turn, so I did. He neglected to say that I should wait until traffic cleared, though, and I turned right into an oncoming stream of cars."

"Whoa, no kidding," Ron said, laughing. "Did you get into an accident?"

"No, I shot off the road and onto the shoulder before anyone hit us," I said, "but your grandfather let me have it with both barrels. I still laugh when I think about the look of absolute horror on Grandpa's face when he saw those cars coming toward us. It's a shame you couldn't have seen it."

"After this afternoon, I think I've got a pretty good idea," Ron said.

"Yeah, I guess you do, Ron. I guess you do."

Therefore, as God's chosen people, holy and dearly loved, clothe yourselves with compassion, kindness, humility, gentleness and patience. Bear with each other and forgive whatever grievances you may have against one another. Forgive as the Lord forgave you.

Colossians 3:12–13

CHAPTER 16

Bring Forth the Royal Diagram

Some men sing in a choir, while others conduct their vocal performances in the privacy of the shower. Me, I sing in the car. I'm the guy you pass on your way to work each morning, oblivious to the world around me, head bobbing, fingers tapping, trying very hard to carry some semblance of a tune. If I see you staring at me through the side window, I stop singing, pick up my cell phone, and pretend to carry on a conversation. But that doesn't fool you.

I don't sing well, but what I lack in pitch and quality, I make up for with deafening volume. Only when I'm alone, of course, with the windows rolled up, and it's still pretty dark outside. If someone is riding along with me, I still sing, but in a mumbling, quiet sort of way—unless, of course, they're family. When we travel as a family, I always draw a number of requests.

"Dad, could you turn the radio up?"

"Do you like this song, Melissa?"

"No, but if it's louder, I won't be able to hear you."

"Dad, will you turn the radio off?"

"Dad, would you please stop singing? You're hurting my ears."

"Dad, slow down so I can jump out."

The kids have a great sense of humor, and they always joke with me like that. Sue even gets involved on occasion, pretending to side with the children by reaching across my lap and blowing the horn at the peak of my performance or plugging her ears in mock contempt. What a bunch of kidders. I play along by raising my voice a decibel or two, which really gets the family going. They love it, though. You can just tell.

I could reduce their criticism if I stopped singing in the car, but that's not likely to happen. Learning the words, or more accurately the correct words, to the songs I sing might help too.

I've enjoyed singing along with the radio for as long as I can remember. A catchy tune comes on, and I join right in. If I know the words, I use them. If I don't, I make them up as I go along, not intentionally or even consciously but out of habit. This becomes the source of some embarrassment when a smart aleck who actually knows the right words overhears my rendition and brings the discrepancy to my attention.

"What did you just say?" Sue asked as we were driving along looking for our first apartment. We were about to be married, and she already felt comfortable enough to poke fun at me.

"I didn't say anything. I was just singing along with the radio."

"But what exactly were you singing?"

"It's Kenny Rogers," I said. "'You Picked a Fine Time to Leave Me, Lucille.' Want me to turn it up?"

"No, no. Go back to the chorus. Sing the chorus again."

Thrilled that my fiancée had finally taken notice of my unique voice, I honored her request and belted out the chorus as I knew it: "You picked a fine time to leave me, Lucille, four hundred children and a clock in the field—"

"Stop. That's the part, right there. Do you realize what you're singing?"

"What?"

"Four hundred children and a clock in the field? That doesn't make any sense. It's 'four hungry children and a crop in the field.'"

"No way."

"Yes way! Think about it. It sounds ridiculous."

This time, she happened to be right, of course, and it opened the door to what has been seventeen years of lyrical corrections, each one bringing her immense joy. I get nervous now when she does listen to me sing because I know she's latched on to another winner.

"Sing that part again," she says.

"No, I don't want to."

"Come on, please!" She laughs, while I try to figure out which words I butchered.

In Bob Seger's "Old Time Rock and Roll," Sue pointed out that "Call me a rebel, call me what you will" probably fit better than my version, "Call me Loretta, call me what you will." It did fit better, and it also put to rest a question I had about Bob Seger.

With Creedance Clearwater Revival's classic, "Bad Moon Rising," she brought to my attention that, considering the title, "There's a bad moon on the rise" was a better line for the chorus than my "There's a bathroom on the right." And for all these years, I had considered it the perfect song for long car trips.

Most recently, Sue caught me singing along to the Doobie Brothers' "What a Fool Believes." At her suggestion, I replaced "She was a grave digger's wife" with "She had a place in his life." It makes for a more upbeat kind of tune.

If there's any consolation to be found, it's that I haven't yet been caught rewriting the classic hymns. With the words right there in front of me, it's a simple matter of reading, and there are no blank spots to fill in. However, I have heard tales of other, more creative minds than mine, overcoming this minor barrier.

"All Hail the Power of Jesus' Name" is a popular target for would be lyricists: "All hail the power of Jesus' name, let angels prostate's fall (ouch!)."

"Bring forth the royal diagram, and crown Him Lord of all." The diagram part I understand. It could easily be understood as the diagram of the heavenly city or Solomon's temple or something along those lines. After all, who ever heard of a diadem or used the word in a sentence?

"Gloria in eggshells Dion" from "Angels We Have Heard on High" sounds completely silly, but to us non-Latin majors, "Gloria in excelsis Deo" doesn't sound a lot better. A neighbor child thought "Come let us adorn him" had something to do with Mary and Joseph dressing the baby Jesus, but the parents have since corrected that discrepancy.

If messing up the lyrics of half-a-dozen songs has done anything positive for me, besides giving my wife a cheap hobby, it is that I am becoming more conscious of both the words I sing and the words I read. It made me realize that more often than not, I sing along without any idea of what the author intended or what the song really means. That might be acceptable when cruising down the street listening to a favorite FM station or cassette (though you can run into a few problems there, as well), but I'm prone to doing exactly the same thing in church.

When the pastor or choir director asks us to stand each Sunday morning, I stand. When he says sit, I sit, and when he says sing, I sing. Until recently, I followed the herd like a mindless cow and didn't pay any attention to the words. I listened to the sermon, that's what I thought I was there for—the lesson.

Oh, occasionally, I was moved by a soloist or a particularly good presentation by the choir, but I think it had more to do with performance than content. I ranked the musical portion of our services as a warm-up to the big show, almost an entertainment during which time latecomers were seated and the rest of us read our bulletins. I'm just starting to realize how much I missed.

If any of this sounds familiar to you, run down to your local Christian bookstore and pick up a hymnal. You might even borrow one from your church. You'll find—like I did—that apart from the Bible, a hymnal contains the most worshipful prose and poetry ever written. Hundreds of love songs proclaim God's glory, sing his praise, and tell his magnificent story. If you can read (not sing, but really read) "How Great Thou Art" straight through without feeling the presence of God, check your pulse and lie down carefully. You may already be dead.

I've gained so much from the lyrics of these hymns that

I've incorporated the hymnal into my quiet time. Some I read, others I offer to God as prayers. Maybe that's what our choir guy means by worshiping through music and what the psalmists meant when they called us to sing with thanksgiving. That would be my guess.

So what shall I do? I will pray with my spirit, but I will also pray with my mind; I will sing with my spirit, but I will also sing with my mind.

1 Corinthians 14:15

CHAPTER 11

A Thanksgiving Recipe

It amazes me to realize how many of my memories are tied to food, although a look in the mirror puts the pieces of the puzzle in place. The sight of a certain pastry in the bakery window sends me decades back; I find myself, once again, holding my father's hand and begging for a dime. One bite of cinnamon toast and I'm sitting at the kitchen table too sick to attend school, but not quite sick enough to forego my mother's coddling. And turkey? That takes me back to my grandmother's house.

As best I can recall, my grandmother's kitchen contained a large, stainless steel oven and absolutely nothing else. I'll admit I probably missed a few things, but for the life of me, I don't remember anything besides that beautiful, shiny, warm oven. Sure, she probably owned a toaster or a blender—a refrigerator at the very least. If so, they escape me as minor tools of an artist whose masterpiece was created in another medium.

Thanksgiving at Grandma's was a Darbee family tradition, and members gathered from the four corners of the world: Brooklyn, Queens, and the north and south shores of Long Island. Aunts and uncles, cousins of the first and second variety, everyone with a remote connection to my father's side was invited and duty bound to attend. Of course, marriages and various ties required some to make only a brief appearance between obligations, but their expressed regrets were undoubtedly heartfelt and sincere. Grandma's house was, without question, the place to be.

Dinner at Grandma's was less a meal than an event. Mashed potatoes and gravy, little gherkin pickles—I always got yelled at for sneaking them from the table before we were officially called to dinner—cranberry sauce, candied yams, and beets—thought to be poisonous, they caused me no temptation whatsoever—were but a few of the many accompaniments to the holiday fare. A juicy, pink ham always graced the table, and a turkey, dark brown and cooked to perfection, was the star attraction. Oh yeah, and rolls. Grandma always made fresh rolls; she wouldn't have dreamed of popping them from a can. A selection of pumpkin, apple, and cherry pies served to motivate the younger, more picky members in the digestion of the aforementioned beets.

The perfect meal certainly wasn't our only Thanksgiving tradition. Serving the meal several hours later than promised ran a close second. Each year, family members received explicit instructions to arrive no later than one o'clock because dinner would be served precisely at two. Apparently,

Grandma claimed Matthew 25:13, "Therefore keep watch, because you do not know the day or the hour," and applied it rather liberally. By three o'clock most of us kids began to get fidgety, and by four, talk of revolt started spreading through the house. When dinner was finally served, sometime in December, I think, the group set about the meal as if ending a forty-day fast.

My cousins and I used this time to take part in yet another time-honored tradition, namely roughhousing, troublemaking, and beating each other senseless. My father and his three siblings were responsible for eight offspring, with not a single "Y" chromosome among them. Eight boys under any one roof are bound to create havoc, and we were never a group to fall short of expectations. Having my bottom warmed—a term that sounds more pleasant, but still means whopped—or standing with my nose in the corner for some length of time was part of that tradition I remember somewhat less fondly.

It wasn't until I married and joined the Marine Corps that I realized how much these traditions meant to me. With more than two thousand miles separating us from our families, Thanksgiving during the early years of our marriage was a quiet and understated affair. Like most young military couples, we didn't have much money. Traveling home for a weekend was so far beyond our budget that it wasn't worthy of consideration. A frozen turkey roll, canned corn, and refrigerator biscuits were the extent of our holiday feast. We both felt something was missing, though good judgment restrained me from saying exactly what, and we began to view Thanksgiving as just another paid holiday.

Then one year in early November, sitting in the living room with a pair of couples we considered our closest friends, someone suggested that we pool our resources and put together an "old-fashioned" Thanksgiving dinner. "The kind my Grandma used to make," somebody suggested. I couldn't have agreed more.

"Why not?" I said, and everyone seemed to agree all at once. Sue volunteered to make pies, someone else signed up for the vegetables, and we all chipped in for a twenty-pound turkey. We started to get excited, and I decided to call home and get my grandmother's recipe for the world's most perfect turkey.

"Grandma," I said into the phone, "can you give me your recipe for Thanksgiving turkey?" The anticipation in my voice was drowned out by the sound of my stomach rumbling.

"Oh, I don't even know what I do," she said. "There's usually a set of instructions on the bag with the bird. Mine always comes out too dry, anyway. Just don't trust those little pop-up thermometers," she continued, "I've never seen one that worked worth a lick."

"Come on, Grandma," I pleaded. "You always make the best turkey. Don't you have some kind of a secret, something you add or do to make it come out just right?"

"It seems to me," Grandma said, "that you've never had a turkey I didn't cook, so I doubt you have much to compare it to." She made a point I had previously failed to consider. "But as it turns out," she said, "I do have a few secrets I'd be willing to share."

"Get yourself a turkey," she continued, "and surround it with the people you love and care about the most. Cook it as slow as humanly possible to give everyone some time to enjoy each other's company, and thank God for every blessing in your lives. I promise you it will be the best Thanksgiving dinner you ever imagined."

As we sat around the table that year—three young

couples—far from our homes and families, someone suggested that we join hands and share with the group the blessings we were most thankful for. Sue and I continue that tradition with our family to this day.

My grandmother's recipe turned out to be a huge success. That meal remains one of my all-time favorites, and the entire evening went off with only one hitch.

"What happened to all the gherkins?" Sue asked as we sat down to begin the dinner. "I put a whole plate of them on the table half an hour ago." She never did find those pickles. They just seemed to disappear. What a strange and unusual thing.

Know that the LORD is God. It is he who made us, and we are his; we are his people, the sheep of his pasture. Enter his gates with thanksgiving and his courts with praise; give thanks to him and praise his name. For the LORD is good and his love endures forever; his faithfulness continues through all generations.

Psalm 100:3–5

CHAPTER 18

A Recipe for Trouble

There wasn't much to do that afternoon, and I'll blame the majority of our problems on the weather. A warm summer storm brought rain to New York and washed away our plans for baseball. We would have played anyway, mind you, but our mothers insisted we remain dry. They also insisted that we sit outside under the awning that hung above the front porch — "No way are you dragging all those kids into my clean house." That quote rang verbatim from six different moms, making me wonder if they shared a manual or, at the very least, compared notes.

Confined to a slab of concrete barely six feet across, we played with the only things our mothers allowed us to carry outside. We played with our imaginations. For a few short minutes, I was Mickey Mantle surrounded by a host of stars. Joltin' Joe DiMaggio sat to the left of me, Roger Maris on my right. Babe Ruth, Lou Gehrig, and "Moose" Skowron filled in the rest of the "dugout" while we waited to see if the umpires would change the status of our rain delay to that of canceled game.

"The Babe is on deck," Tony "Lou Gehrig" Gianelli announced from his position beside our imaginary home plate. "Let me knock this one over the wall, and then you're up."

Elliot "Babe Ruth" Pelzman took exception to the idea, however, preferring to come to the plate with at least one runner on, thereby boosting his RBI average. "Just hit a single, Tony, so I can bring you in." Here lies one of the great problems of imaginary baseball: Everybody hits home runs. In the twenty or thirty minutes we had been playing the game, we racked up a score of twenty-three to nothing with no outs, top of the first. If it didn't stop raining soon, we'd all be in the Hall of Fame before twilight.

"This is crazy," somebody complained. "Nobody gets a homer every time at bat. Strike out this time or at least hit a grounder. I'm tired of listening to 'Going . . . going . . . gone . . . goodbye!'"

"The Iron Horse never strikes out," Tony informed us. "Lou Gehrig got on base every time he came up."

"Nobody gets on base every time, Tony," I argued. "Gehrig had hundreds of strikeouts, just like everyone else."

"Never happened," Tony returned.

"If a player got on base every time he swung the bat," Artie joined in, "the Yanks would have to pay him a million dollars a year or something" (a great deal of money back then). Nowadays, a million dollars wouldn't buy the Yankees a utility infielder capable of hitting the ground if he passed out.

It was obvious to me that this game had run its course. So with the oratory skills of a practiced statesman, I expressed my dissatisfaction and recommended we seek an alternative entertainment. "This stinks. Let's do something else."

"Like what?" Artie asked.

"I don't know, anything," I answered. "We could pretend to be astronauts or G-men or something."

"That's stupid!" Tony shot out.

"You're stupid!" Elliot came to my defense.

"Your mother's stupid," and Tony barely got the words out of his mouth before Elliot landed on top of him. This was nothing unusual; in fact, most days included one or another of us at least considering the idea of throttling Tony. While I drew the line at consideration, Elliot often brought the concept to fruition. When we grew tired of watching Elliot rub his knuckles through Tony's scalp (officially called a "noogie"), we pulled the two apart and continued contemplating our next activity.

"We could flip cards," I suggested. Flipping baseball cards was a popular pastime when Topps was the card of choice, and adults hadn't ruined the hobby by assigning a monetary value to the cardboard. They came in packs of ten and included a stick of gum that shattered into razor-edged shards on exposure to the air. You could cut glass with the gum if diamonds weren't available or, at the very least, slice the inside of your mouth.

"Naw, it's too wet," Tony whined. "I don't feel like running through the rain to get my cards."

"Well, then what do you want to do?" someone asked, and we now had all of the ingredients for disaster: Mix six parts boredom with equal parts of imagination, add water (in this case rain), season with time and opportunity, and allow the mixture to settle until trouble rises to the top.

"Why don't we go see a movie?" Tony suggested. Familiar calls of "I don't have any money" and "We don't even know what's playing" followed.

"So what?" Tony said. "We only need enough for one ticket."

Buy one, get five free. I remember thinking that had to be one of the best matinee deals in the city. Hard to believe a theater could stay in business offering their customers such incredible bargains. However, once Tony elaborated on the details of the offer, the economics became clearer.

"If we all chip in," Tony explained, "and come up with enough money for one ticket, the rest of us can sneak in through the back."

"The back doors are always locked," Elliot said. "How are we supposed to sneak in?"

Tony had that part figured out, also. "The doors are only locked from the outside," he explained. "They can't lock them from the inside because it's a fire exit. What we do is send one guy in with enough money to buy a ticket, and he opens the back door for the rest of us. My sister does it all the time."

"Does your sister ever get caught?" Artie asked.

"Never," Tony assured us. "Whoever opens the door just has to wait until the usher heads into the snack bar. Then, as soon as the door opens, we rush in and scatter."

Everyone agreed the idea had merit. Only one minor ethical point troubled me, and I brought it to the group's attention. "Isn't this sort of like stealing?" I asked. "I mean, if six of us watch the movie, aren't we supposed to buy six tickets?" Not surprisingly, Tony had an answer for this, too.

"It's only stealing," he explained, "if you take something that doesn't belong to you. Snatch a box of candy or some licorice ropes from the counter, and that qualifies as stealing.

This is more like taking advantage of an opportunity. We're not costing them any money," Tony continued. "They're gonna show the movie anyway. We're just filling in the empty seats."

I still wasn't completely comfortable with the idea, but since I found myself in the awkward position as the group's only dissenter, I gave in to the will of my peers and agreed to come along with only one stipulation. "If the theater's crowded," I informed my friends, "and it looks like I'm taking someone's seat, I'm leaving." This was my attempt to take a stand on the moral high ground and rationalize my actions. As long as I wasn't keeping a paying customer from watching the movie, I could justify sneaking into the theater. I doubt it was my first foray into the world of situational ethics, but it is the one I most often remember.

We collected our loose change and appointed Tony to act as the inside man, since the idea belonged to him and through association with his sister he possessed the closest thing to experience. Following a wet and brisk four-block run to the theater, we paused to catch our breaths and talked strategy one last time.

"Remember, as soon as I open the door, run in and grab a seat," Tony reminded us. "Don't worry about where it is or who's in front of you, just sit down. We can pick out better seats once everything calms down."

"What if we get caught?" I asked.

"You won't," Tony said, "but if you do, I don't know you." His sense of loyalty moved me beyond description.

As Tony disappeared around the corner to purchase "our" ticket, I battled one last round with my conscience. What we were about to do was wrong; I knew this without question. But everyone else seemed fine with the idea, and while Tony's arguments hadn't truly convinced me of our innocence, they had managed to soften the guilt. It appeared that sound judgment and personal conviction would give in to peer pressure when the door flew suddenly open.

"Come on!" Tony yelled. "Hurry up!"

Just as we had discussed, I ran as soon as the door opened. Contrary to the plan, however, I ran in the opposite direction—as hard and fast as my feet would carry me. Admittedly as much from fear of retribution as a sense of right and wrong, I chickened out at the last minute and beat a path straight for home. With each step I imagined my friends' anger and thought about the abuse I'd receive for my cowardly act. The words *chicken* and *sissy* came immediately to mind, but then I heard *it:* Without missing a step, I glanced over my shoulder to investigate what sounded like applause, but "it" turned out to be eight rubber soles pounding the wet pavement in hot pursuit. It was worse than I thought. They had to be awfully angry to chase me all the way home and give up on the movie. I continued running, hoping to make the safety of my front porch (they wouldn't beat me too bad on my own porch) before the incensed mob overtook me.

With only a slight lead, I reached my objective three or four paces before my pursuers, grabbed the iron railing, and pulled myself up to the porch in one motion. I turned quickly to face my former friends, preferring to see the attack coming rather than getting caught from behind.

"That was great!" Elliot yelled as they all piled under our awning. "Really cool." "Good idea ditching Tony," Artie congratulated me. "I wish I thought of it. Next time let us in on it, will ya?"

Caught off guard and a bit confused, I tried to sort out the accolades coming my way. My friends weren't angry at all. In fact, they were under the impression that I had instigated a practical joke. Whether my act was born of cowardice or conscience never entered the conversation. We laughed and joked and speculated as whether Tony was enjoying the movie. The majority's opinion believed he was not.

The guys gave me quite a bit to think about that afternoon, and as I lay in bed that evening, I wondered about my response to peer pressure. While I eventually made the right decision, at least to some degree, I found it all too easy to put aside what I knew was right for what looked more appealing. When faced with a question of black or white, I sought the gray area and tried to justify my actions in order to satisfy my desires.

Another point absolutely fascinated me — running away caused a chain reaction. The moment I ran, four pairs of feet charged after me. It could be that everyone believed I was playing a joke on Tony, but more likely, they shared my apprehensions and were looking for an opportunity to back out. I often wonder how many times I've laid better judgment aside in order to be part of the group when all the group needed was better judgment. It is a lesson I find myself learning again and again.

No temptation has seized you except what is common to man. And God is faithful; he will not let you be tempted beyond what you can bear. But when you are tempted, he will also provide a way out so that you can stand up under it.

1 Corinthians 10:13

CHAPTER 19

Widgets, Gadgets, and General Gizmos

"Reach up in the cupboard above the sink and pull out the blender," I directed my son as I chopped fruit for the evening's dessert. The strawberry crepes were an extra-credit project assigned by Ron's French teacher, and our family served as the official taste testers—or guinea pigs, depending on your frame of reference. Since my work history included a number of restaurants during my teenage years (including Café la Crepe), I received the honor of assisting our novice chef with the preparation and assembly. This was not one of the bonding experiences I had anticipated, but an opportunity, nonetheless.

"Oh, shoot!" Ron yelled as he opened the cupboard and a hundred or so homeless Tupperware lids tumbled out of the cabinet—some coming to an immediate rest, others rolling aimlessly about the kitchen counters and floor.

"The other cupboard above the sink, Ron," I said, "not the one with all the Tupperware lids."

"No kidding, Dad. Thanks for the advice," he said, and chased after a rogue lid rolling in circles around a leg of the kitchen table.

"Just get me the blender," I repeated. "You can pick up this mess when we're finished."

Ron opened the other cabinet, but ran into some difficulty finding the blender. "Is this it?" he asked, holding up the mini-Cuisinart.

"No, that's a food processor."

"How about this?" and he offered me the chopper/grater attachment we received as an added bonus.

"Try another cupboard," I suggested.

His search turned up a variety of appliances: bread maker, pasta machine, ice cream freezer, and combination rice cooker/vegetable steamer, but not a blender in sight. Only slightly annoyed, I stopped chopping and joined in the hunt. We found an iced tea maker, two hand mixers, a slow cooker, deep fryer, Sno-Cone machine, and a waffle iron, but still no blender. I went into a slow boil as we ferreted out a jet-stream oven I forgot we even owned, Salad Shooter, pretzel maker, pressure cooker, and a contraption for pulling the lids from stubborn jars. Thankfully, the cookie gun wasn't loaded or I might have done something foolish.

"Sue!" I yelled, convinced that this problem had gotten out of hand and determined to do something about it. "Could you come in here, please?"

"Need some help?" she asked.

"Yeah, we need some help," I said. "We need some help

finding the stinking blender. This kitchen looks like a warehouse for Ron Popeil! How did you ever let it get this way?"

She pulled the blender out from behind the food dehydrator, handed it to Ron, and turned to answer my question. "Don't blame this mess on me" fell short of the weeping confession of guilt and promise of repentance I was looking for.

"What do you mean, 'Don't blame this mess on me?'" I questioned. "You're in charge of the kitchen. We have enough appliances to open our own trade show in here."

"I didn't buy any of it" was the only lame excuse she came up with.

"I know you didn't buy this stuff," I said, "but why did you ever let *me* buy this junk?"

"Why did I *let* you buy this junk?" she asked. "I guess it's some kind of character flaw. How am I supposed to stop you? Should I physically drag you out of the warehouse stores or pull the plug during the next infomercial?"

Realizing the problem might not be totally Sue's fault, I tried putting an end to our suddenly unpleasant conversation. "Never mind," I said. "Thanks for the blender. We'll have dinner ready in half an hour."

I'm starting to face the fact that I have a problem. I'm addicted to gadgets—and not just kitchen gadgets but anything with a cord or batteries that promises to perform better, faster, easier, or with more versatility. I guess that's not completely true; I've bought a few solar-operated toys and a wind-powered generator that caught my eye too. I admit, I find it difficult to resist the latest innovations. I'm attracted to technological advancements whether I need them or not.

Our vacuum cleaner can pick up a fifteen-pound bowling

ball and hold it in the air indefinitely, inflate a four-person life raft in under four minutes, and includes an attachment for grooming the cat. The instructions don't include any information about convincing a cat to allow such grooming — ours hides under the bed the minute we kick start this contraption — but if we figure that out, we'll have the cleanest cat in Northern California. What the vacuum won't do is pull the really tough stuff out of carpet, like paper clips, dirt, or lint. Sue reminds me of that purchase no less than once a week.

My ceiling fan came with a remote control, our heating and air-conditioning run on a digital timer. The lawn sprinklers operate on seven different stations, and I can set the duration of each individually. Our computer responds to my voice, and my answering system pages me with my messages. Clap and the lights come on, whistle and our key rings beep in response. There is no gizmo too small, no contraption too ridiculous, to draw my attention.

After dinner, while we enjoyed our strawberry crepes, I made a pledge. "I've been thinking about all the junk we've accumulated," I said, "and I'm ready to do something about it. This spring we'll have a yard sale, and anything we don't use goes in it. And from now on," I continued, "no more impulse buying. From this point forward, I'm done listening to every promise of bigger, better, faster, quieter. I'm a new man." That drew a hearty "We'll see" from Sue, but I was serious and determined to change.

I quit, cold turkey, for three full months. Not so much as a pocket calculator entered our home. Smokers wear a nicotine patch, and I tried gluing a UPC sticker on my arm, but it didn't help much. I avoided all of my old haunts — the computer trade shows, Radio Shack, and the electronics megastores. After twelve weeks, I was still clean, completely gadget-free . . . until I fell asleep in my chair.

The Bulls were on television when I nodded off, but I awoke to the luring sounds of Chet and Bridgette peddling a vacuum-sealing system guaranteed to change my life. They sealed meat and vegetables for storage in the freezer, dried goods for improved shelf life, and liquids to store away for times of emergency. "Like to go camping?" Chet asked. "Vacuum seal entire meals and carry them along with you!" The convincing couple even showed footage of their white-water rafting trip and how they vacuum-sealed everything in their packs to keep things dry. The shot of Chet's underwear floating down river—just as dry as the Sahara desert—after an overturn on the rapids almost convinced me.

"But wait!" Bridgette said, and I waited. "Show our friends what we're going to give them for buying this amazing product today!" Chet showed us a special attachment for sealing mason jars for home canning, resealing open wine bottles, and keeping the carbonation in two-liter bottles of soda. Still, they weren't finished. The first two hundred callers would receive a copy of Bridgette's book, *Living a Vacuum-Full Life.* The hook came when they graciously offered to make the first payment for me.

I grabbed a pencil and paper and jotted down the 800 number flashing across my screen. Taking the portable phone, I dialed the operator, who was standing by to assist me, and waited on hold because my business was important to them, and I would be serviced by the next available representative. Chet and Bridgette continued their demonstration while I waited.

"Who are you talking to?" Sue asked as she came into the living room.

"Ahh, no one, really," I said.

She must have recognized the guilt on my face, and she glanced at the television to see Chet vacuum-sealing a small foreign sports car as the grand finale. "You would probably never do this at home," Bridgette said, "but if this amazing item can seal a vintage Porsche, just think what it will do for your vegetables!"

"Fight it!" Sue encouraged me. "Put down the phone, and say no to useless gadgets."

"You don't understand," I pleaded. "This one's different. This one's going to change our lives. I'm buying this for us. We're going to live vacuum full!"

"Put down the phone, or you'll feel awful tomorrow."

"I can't. I've tried. I need this one, Sue. Let me have just this one."

"It's up to you," she said. "I can't make this decision for you. But think about the Sno-Cone Magician collecting dust out there in the cupboard before you make up your mind. I think you know what you have to do."

Sue left the room, and I continued to watch Chet and Bridgette as I waited on hold. They showed the documented savings for an average family of four living a vacuum-full life. I couldn't afford not to own one, they said. It was an investment that would pay for itself.

"Thank you for waiting. How can I help you?" the operator interrupted the elevator music playing through my phone. "I'm interested in the Incredible, Amazing Vacuum Maniac," I told the operator. "Does it have a money-back guarantee?"

"It most certainly does, sir. May I take your order?"

"Does it come with a warranty?" I asked.

"One year parts and labor," she answered. "May I take your order?"

"Well, does it have a timer, so that I can set it before I go to bed and vacuum-seal stuff while I'm sleeping?"

"No, Sir, but I can't imagine why anyone would want to do that."

"Too bad, because I do," I said. "Thanks anyway. Maybe some other time." I hung up the phone and basked for a moment in my victory. Walking into the kitchen, I shared the good news with Sue.

"Well, get used to food spoiling, soda going flat, and wet clothes on rafting trips," I said, "because I didn't buy it."

"We have two teenagers," Sue said. "Food doesn't last long enough to spoil, and soda never goes flat. As for rafting, I'm willing to take that risk."

"Good," I said.

"You know, I'm proud of you," Sue complimented.

"I'm proud of me too," I said. "I think I finally licked this thing. Hey, what's that you've got in the bag?"

"It's nothing. Just leave it there, and I'll pick it up later."

I walked over to the counter and opened the bag, pulling out the single item it contained and holding it up for inspection. "This looks like a universal remote control to me," I said. "Is there something you'd like to tell me?"

"Don't get any ideas," Sue said. "It was supposed to be a gift, because you were doing so well. I thought you might like it."

"Thanks anyway, Dear," I said, "but maybe you should take it back. I don't want to tempt myself."

And besides, who wants one remote control when you can

have six of them piled next to your chair. There are some things she'll never understand.

See to it that no one takes you captive through hollow and deceptive philosophy, which depends on human tradition and the basic principles of this world rather than on Christ. For in Christ all the fullness of the Deity lives in bodily form, and you have been given fullness in Christ, who is the head over every power and authority.

Colossians 2:8–10

CHAPTER 20

Sports Channel Junkie

**Sports on TV Makes a Glorious Day
(To the tune of "These Are a Few of
My Favorite Things")**

NFL football fills my screen on Sunday,
Frank Gifford brings me the big game on Monday;
Offense and defense and special teams play—
Sports on TV makes a glorious day.

Tuesday brings basketball, soccer, or hockey,
Wednesday's that special on triple-crown jockeys;
Costas just interviewed quick Sugar Ray—
Sports on TV makes a glorious day.

Tee off on Thursday with Golf Channel previews,
Close out my Friday with Sports Center's reviews;

Sportscasters always have something to say—
Sports on TV makes a glorious day.

Chorus:
College football
On the last day
Makes my week run smooth;
I set my remote for ESPN2,
And then I don't need to move.

I can recite the starting lineup for Gil Hodges's 1969 New York Mets. No one ever asked me to, but the knowledge is there, nonetheless, stored away and ready to impress should the opportunity ever present itself.

As a youngster, I sat with my dad and watched every play of the '69 World Series, from the opening pitch until Cleon Jones caught the final fly ball. My shoulders sagged in dejection as Tom Seaver dropped game one. I soared with elation as his teammates rallied to grab the next four straight from Frank Robinson and the Baltimore Orioles. Right from the pages of a storybook, the frogs of the National League turned into royal princes. That's when it happened. That's when I got hooked.

It started innocently enough. A baseball game here and there, an occasional night of hockey, even a college bowl game if the teams matched up. I could take it or leave it—no problem. I didn't need to watch sports; I *chose* to. It's not like I was addicted.

As the years progressed, so did the yearning. Seasons began to blend together—basketball, hockey, football. By 1986, when the Mets won their next World Series, the warning signs began to appear—falling asleep in front of the television and rushing home early to catch a play-off game. A weekend feeding no longer satisfied the hunger; I needed more.

Saturday and Sunday binges led into Monday Night Football and Tuesday night wrap-ups. Before long, I was supporting a seven-day-per-week habit. ESPN and the Sports Channel were mainlined throughout the house. Twin Zeniths adorned the living room, one atop the other so I wouldn't miss a game.

Finally, I hit bottom. Financially overextended after purchasing the seven-foot, rear-projection TV (with surround sound and picture-in-picture), the minisatellite dish, and the NFL grandstand package (thirteen games every Sunday), I could no longer afford to make my Pay-Per-View obligations. The cable police showed up at our door and demanded their converter box. One of them reached toward my line with a pair of wire cutters. I grabbed the line . . . there was a struggle . . . and then. . . .

"Hey! Wake up," my wife said, shaking me. "What's the matter?"

"Don't take the antenna," I said. "The antenna's mine!"

"Will you please wake up," Sue repeated. "What's the matter with you?"

"Oh, wow. It must have been a dream. I think I had a nightmare," I said, starting to shake off the fog. "It was horrible. The cable company came and took away our converter box and big-screen TV."

"We don't have a converter box or a big-screen TV," my wife said. "Could it be you're still thinking about missing Sunday school to watch that football game tomorrow?"

So there it was. I had talked about ducking out of church early the next morning—going in for the first service and skipping Sunday school to watch the Giants whip up on the Cowboys. What could it hurt? We're talking one Sunday here, not a lifetime. I went to bed mulling the idea over in my mind, trying to justify something I knew was wrong. Apparently my conscience worked overtime to keep me on track, and it got me thinking.

Televised sporting events account for a fairly large chunk of my entertainment time. Could it be that I'm spending too much time with the boys in the booth? When it comes to sports on TV, is there too much? Is it possible to be addicted to sports?

For starters, I looked up the word *addicted* in my dictionary. American Heritage defines *addicted* as: "To devote or give [oneself] habitually or compulsively." Well, that certainly doesn't pertain to me. So confident was I that I sought independent verification.

"Honey, this doesn't sound like me, does it?"

"No-o-o-o-o-o, uh-uh, absolutely not." She shook her head from side to side in an exaggerated motion and walked back into the family room laughing that evil laugh she reserves for these occasions.

"Wait a minute, now," I said, following behind her. "I don't watch sports habitually."

"Absolutely not, Dear," she answered. "Not unless you consider every Monday night football game, the Mets' and Knicks' televised schedules, the Rangers (if they happen to be doing well) and occasional college games a habit."

"OK, I see how it might give the impression of a habit, but no way am I compulsive." The corners of her mouth twitched slightly, and I could see the evil laugh creeping toward the surface. "Come on now; admit it," I said. "You know I'm not compulsive."

"Sweetheart, you talk to the television."

"I do not talk to the television."

"You most certainly do," she said. "When a ref makes a bad call or a play gets really exciting, you leap out of the recliner, land on your knees in front of the set, and scream at the screen." As if to hammer the point home she threw her hands in the air and demonstrated, "Go-Go-Go-Go-Go-o-o-o-o-o-o. You know, just like you did in Lamaze class." Boy, she looked silly doing that.

"So I talk to the TV when I get excited. At least I don't claim to hear it talking back. That doesn't make me compulsive."

"Would you prefer *obsessive*?"

"I'd prefer *charming* and *debonair*, but the conversation doesn't seem to be heading in that direction." Feeling somewhat defeated and painfully aware of yet another shortcoming, I headed for the relative safety of the study. I left the television off just to prove I could.

So just where does a guy draw the line when it comes to sports viewing habits? Refrain altogether? I certainly hope not, and I find no biblical evidence to support that conclusion. We all need some degree of rest and relaxation. The secret lies in staying on that side of the line marked "fan" and remaining several feet back from the side marked "fanatic."

Try the following five-question quiz to get an idea of where you line up when it comes to sports on TV.

Question #1:

Your wife's dearly loved and recently departed Aunt Ursula bequeaths to her an extensive and valuable collection of Hummel figurines. How do you respond?

A. Give up your plans to watch college football on Saturday to go down into the basement and build a new curio shelf.

B. Do nothing, knowing that once your wife has experienced a reasonable period of grief, she will be better suited to deal with such a trivial issue.

C. Suggest she sell the Hummels and put the money toward something the family can use.

D. Pawn the elfish-looking glass trinkets and buy a really cool entertainment system and one of those armchair quarterback remote control holders.

Question #2:

Left at home with the children during game two of the World Series, you notice the baby has soiled yet another diaper and is in serious need of changing. Being the great dad that you are, what do you do?

A. Change your son during the next commercial.

B. Wait for the seventh inning stretch.

C. Give his older sister two bucks and point her toward the offending odor.

D. Put the baby in that swing contraption at the other end of the house and hope he falls asleep.

Question #3:

What does your normal bedtime ritual consist of?

A. Reading a few passages of Scripture before nodding off.

B. Marking tomorrow's sports shows in *TV Guide*.

C. Setting the VCR to record an important sporting event like the Brazilian jai alai championships on ESPN.

D. Wishing you didn't have to go to work tomorrow, so that you could stay up and watch an important sporting event like the Brazilian jai alai championships on ESPN.

Question #4:

How would you finish the following sentence? When John Madden starts drawing those X's and O's on the screen, I . . .

A. Wonder if he missed a dose of medication.

B. Try to follow along as best I can.

C. Understand everything he is trying to communicate.

D. Grab my dry erase markers and join right in.

Question #5:

When do you usually watch a sporting event?

A. With my family or a few close friends.

B. Alone.

C. In the breakroom at work.

D. On my Sony Watchman while I operate a lathe and other heavy machinery for my job in the nuclear power industry.

Scoring: Give yourself three points for each "D" answer, two points for each "C," one point for every "B" you chose, and zero for each "A."

If you scored:

0 points:	Don't worry. You exhibit none of the behavior normally associated with sports addiction. You might be interested to know, however, that the Dodgers moved to Los Angeles.
1–5 points:	Sports viewing habits seem to be under control.
6–10 points:	Remember that line between "fan" and "fanatic." Look down, you may be straddling it.

11–15 points: Are you one of those guys who paints his body with the team colors and sits in the stands bare-chested on subfreezing January afternoons?

So, maybe you scored pretty well, and then again, maybe you didn't. It's entirely possible that you have your life together more than I do, or maybe sports aren't your thing, and something else takes up a disproportionate amount of your time. The point is, if left unchecked, almost anything we do harbors the potential for abuse. As men and women of Christ, we are accountable for our time, and how we use our time reflects heavily on what we believe. (Remember the saying, "Show me a man's calendar and his checkbook, and I'll tell you what's important to him.")

Is there anything wrong with watching sports on TV? No, we all need relaxation. Great freedom exists for those of us in Christ, and great choices. Along with the freedom to choose how we will relax comes the responsibility to choose wisely. And I'd be willing to guess it was just as difficult before they brought us twenty-four-hour sports networks.

Do you not know that those who run in a race all run, but one receives the prize? And everyone who competes for the prize is temperate in all things. Now they do it to obtain a perishable crown, but we for an imperishable crown.

1 Corinthians 9:24–25 (NKJV)

CHAPTER 21

The Things Men Never Say

"Does this look good on me?" I don't know what Sue was wearing, but price tags hung from it, and if I know Sue, it was probably on sale.

"Sure," I responded without looking up from the magazine I purchased especially for this trip to the mall.

"How do you know?" Sue asked. "You're not even looking."

"I know you," I said. "You have impeccable taste, and I'm sure whatever it is looks lovely." I glanced up briefly just to satisfy her and said, "See that, lovely. I knew it all the time."

"Why do I even take you shopping?" Sue asked. "You are absolutely no help."

"I don't know, Sue. I always figured it was some sort of punishment."

"For me or for you?"

"If you feel that way about it, I'll stay home next time," I volunteered.

"And miss all this excitement? We couldn't have that, now, could we?"

I recognize a rhetorical question when I hear one. Actually, I don't mind going shopping with Sue too much. It gives us a chance to get out together for a little while, and I usually pick the spot for lunch—one of the enticements she offers me. Besides, watching people shop of a short course in human nature, and I can always use the education.

I'm convinced that most men don't really know how to shop, at least not for clothes or shoes and stuff. We know how to shop for cars. Maybe it's because clothes seem too inconsequential.

When Sue shops, she does so without a specific target in mind. She may look seriously at fifteen or twenty items over the course of an afternoon, try on five, and purchase one or two. She doesn't do this excessively, maybe every month or so, but she does it much more often than I do.

I shop for clothes once or twice a year, and then only when I can no longer bear the criticisms directed toward my wardrobe from my wife and daughter. I keep a specific target in mind, say pants. I find a pair that fits, and I buy them. Sue then rushes in and finds me a matching shirt, socks, and possibly a tie.

It's not unusual for me to select a pair of pants on one of these annual jaunts and head to the counter with three or four pairs, same style, same manufacturer, but different colors. This absolutely gives Sue fits.

"You can't buy all the same pants," she says.

"Why not? They're different colors."

"But they're all the same."

"Do you like this pair?" I ask, holding one up for her to inspect.

"Yes, but—"

"Then you oughta love these," I say.

"At least try them on," Sue always asks.

"Honey, they're the same. If this pair fits, chances are pretty good the rest fit too." And off she goes to find the matching shirts, because I'm not allowed to do that part. Rumor has it that I suffer a deficit of taste, thus embarrassing my wife and daughter with my selections.

I don't ask, "How does this look on me?" I never question if something makes me look fat. In fact, there are a lot of things women say—shopping or otherwise—that you aren't likely to hear coming from the mouths of men.

"This color brings out the blue in my eyes," is one that comes readily to mind. "I don't have the shoes for this outfit," follows closely behind.

"Am I still pretty?" "Let's just cuddle," and "What you need is a good long cry" all make the list. Men not only refrain from saying these things, they don't know how to respond when the women in their lives do.

"Can you believe Sam wore that shirt to the party?" A guy just wouldn't say that, and unless Sam's shirt was day-glo orange, chances are pretty good a man won't remember the shirt at all. "Sam had a shirt?" a guy will respond.

I get myself into trouble trying to answer questions like that on a regular basis. "How do you really *feel* about the drapes?" Sue asked me once.

"I don't *feel* anything about them," I said. "They're drapes. I feel that they'll cover the window."

"But do you like them?" Sue asked. "Do you really like them?"

"They're just drapes," I said. "I don't feel a personal attachment to them, if that's what you mean. If anything, I *feel* they're a little expensive." This fits into the category of insensitive, or so I've been told.

The real biggie, though, *numero uno* on the list of things you'll never hear a man say, is: "Why don't you ever say 'I love you' anymore?" Admittedly, we're probably afraid of the answer. But this is a popular line with women.

My grandmother used to ask my grandfather that question from time to time. He always responded with, "I told you that when I married you. If something changes, I'll let you know." I doubt the line was original—I've heard it a hundred times since then—but I always found a degree of logic in those words, even if I know better than to repeat them.

Yes, there are a lot of things men never say, or more accurately, don't say easily. Some of them are a source of humor, others cause us a lot of problems. I have an incredibly difficult time saying, "I need some help over here." History shows that I'm more likely to screw something up and make that point obvious than I am to ask for help—especially if the problem is of an emotional or relational nature.

"Your will be done, Lord," used to give me a great deal of trouble. I said the words, all right—almost by rote, but they often came with a caveat or further instructions just in case Almighty God wasn't clear on my desires. "Your will be done, Lord, but I'd prefer to have it this way . . ." and I'd explain my preferences to God. What I really said was, "My will be done, God, and I'd appreciate it if you'd line your will up with mine so we can get down to business." But we all know God doesn't work that way.

Several years ago, our son, Ron, became ill for an extended period of time. What we thought was a mild flu went on for days and then weeks. Weeks turned into months, and

Ron was in and out of Children's Hospital, undergoing tests and exploratory surgeries. I prayed every day that God would bring healing to my son. I prayed for faith, and I prayed for patience. Every prayer ended with, "Your will be done, Lord," but I didn't truly mean that.

I was more afraid during those months than I've ever been in my life. I petitioned God for immediate healing, and couldn't comprehend why his will might allow Ron's illness to continue any longer. The doctors ran out of ideas, and our son still wasn't responding to treatment. I prayed and I pleaded, I begged and I cried, and, eventually, I came to a point where I could honestly say, "Your will be done, Lord." I didn't have any other options; I was forced to trust God.

And God healed Ron. We never found out exactly what was wrong with him, but his problems ended almost overnight. It seemed to me that God was waiting for me to trust him, so that he could resolve the situation. I wish I hadn't waited so long.

My natural inclination is not to seek God's guidance but to act, and react to the situations before me and do the follow-up work with God later. I sometimes forget that he is my Guide and Master, and I treat God as a holy fireman, expecting him to put out the brush fires I've managed to stir up.

"Your will be done, Lord," are the five hardest words I've ever learned to say, and I think they're just about as difficult for most men. Truthfully, I still have a rough time with them on occasion, and catch myself trying to barter with God. Sometimes it takes time to remember that God loves me, and his will for me is good and perfect, before I can say those words and honestly mean them.

That still leaves a lot of things men will never say, and

many of them with good reason. "Am I still pretty?" I asked the guy I carpool with while we drove to work one morning.

"What? Are you nuts?" Jerry yelled.

"No," I said. "It's just one of those things you never hear a guy ask, and I thought I'd bring it up for discussion. So, what do you think?"

"I think you're delusional. That's what I think." He never actually answered my question. I guess there are some things men never say.

Be joyful always; pray continually; give thanks in all circum-

stances, for this is God's will for you in Christ Jesus.

1 Thessalonians 5:16–18

CHAPTER 22

The School of Hard Knocks

When you are fortunate enough to have an older brother, life simply overflows with advantages. For one thing, you never need to worry about where your next beating will come from because the biggest, meanest, most relentless bully you know is waiting for you at home. Add to that the privilege of a hand-me-down wardrobe, teachers who have preconceived opinions about your attitude, with absolutely no chance of ever getting dibs on the front seat, and life pretty nearly reaches perfection.

My older brother, Jimmy, and I shared a mutually beneficial relationship growing up, wherein he used me to refine the art of felonious assault, while I, in turn, bled profusely for his enjoyment. But don't for a minute believe that the fun stopped there.

At the insistence of my older brother, I became the guinea pig for every lamebrain idea he came up with. Like a canary sent into the shaft ahead of miners, I was the first to walk over makeshift bridges, a pioneer for underground tunnels, and an all-around expendable resource if something gave the slightest appearance of danger. Never one to hog the lime-light, Jimmy graciously allowed me to take the blame for all of his mischief, and on occasion, even made up some extra blame to make sure my parents didn't neglect me. His love for me ran very deep.

Our relationship wasn't all pain and discomfort. After all, my brother was human, for the most part, and between as-sassination attempts, the maniac had to eat and sleep just like sane people. Sometimes, finding himself too exhausted to give me a proper beating, Jimmy would take the time to mentor and teach me. Under his guiding hand, I learned to hold my breath underwater for two full minutes, developed lighten-ing-quick reflexes, and became one of the fastest sprinters in my age group. Jimmy was a true educator.

Regardless of the injury my brother attempted to inflict on my person, I always knew I could find protection in my par-ents' arms. As the baby of the family, my safety was guaran-teed at the hem of my mother's apron or the foot of my father's chair. Once, when Jimmy was showing me how he could cut off a human head with a garrote (thankfully, he couldn't get his hands on any piano wire and had to settle for a terry cloth towel), I managed to escape to the safety of my mother's kitchen.

"Mom, Jimmy's trying to cut my head off with a towel!" I screamed, seeking her immediate intervention. Mom laid into Jimmy right then and there, putting a stop to his psy-chopathic behavior.

"Stop teasing your brother," she scolded. "Now the two of

you run along and play nice." That was nearly as effective as asking Lizzie Borden to quit fooling around with sharp objects.

"Now I'm gonna hurt you," Jimmy mumbled, as soon as we were out of earshot. As I understood his logic, the penalty for attempting to avoid death at his hand was a thorough beating, which—to me, anyway—seemed a reasonable trade off.

In his own twisted way, my older brother also offered me some protection from the dangers of life outside of our home. It was common knowledge around the neighborhood that I was Jimmy's property, and nobody dared mess with his property without obtaining permission. In order to hit me, they were required to first acquire my brother's authorization. While he proved extremely benevolent in doling out this privilege, few ever asked. They probably figured the sport was already beaten out of me.

At some point in my youth, I began to wonder how my parents even tolerated my older brother. I know that I was finding it a difficult task. His lack of attributes was evident enough, and I figured they kept him around out of a sense of responsibility. Certainly they didn't feel the same overwhelming love and affection for him as they so obviously felt for me. I had to give them credit, though. They were doing a marvelous job of hiding their disdain.

When my mother came into my room to tuck me in one evening, I decided to offer my services as a confidant and provide her with an outlet to vent her pent-up frustrations. Already sure of the answer I would receive, I asked her which one of her sons she loved the most.

"Who do you love more, me or Jimmy?" I asked. I hated to put her on the spot like that, but I felt it would be good for her to vocalize her feelings. I didn't doubt for a moment that she would profess a strong bias in my favor. The question was what you might call a "no-brainer," a choice between her loving, charming, incredibly cute baby boy and the demon spawn who lurked in the adjoining bedroom.

"I love you both equally," my mother answered, and her response absolutely floored me. It wasn't that I actually believed her, but to hear such a boldface lie from my dear mother's lips, even if it was to spare my brother's feelings, disturbed me deeply.

"Come on, Mom. You can tell me the truth," I said. "I won't tell Jimmy."

"I am telling you the truth," she said. "You are both my sons, and I love you both equally."

"But Jimmy's an animal, Mom," I argued. "He's not very nice, he beats me up, and, I'm not sure, but I think he might be a Communist." My course of reasoning did little to sway my mother's opinion.

"I know he picks on you sometimes, but he's not that bad," she defended. "Besides, I don't love either of you because of the things you do or don't do. I love you because you are my children, and while I might not always like the things you do, I will always love you." Personally, I found her logic a bit difficult to follow.

Nowadays, my brother and I share a much different relationship. Time and maturity have a way of changing the way siblings interact. He hasn't beaten me up in almost twenty years. Of course, he stopped growing a full six inches shy of the height I attained, but I don't think that had much to do with it.

Now that I see my brother in a different light, and also have children of my own, it's much easier to understand my mother's view of love. And her unconditional love for her sons has helped me develop an understanding of God's love.

I often wondered how a holy and righteous God could love me. With all of my faults and through all of my disobedience, he continues to love me and keep me as his own. When you make as many mistakes as I do, that can be a difficult concept to follow. Thankfully, I had an early example that continues to remind me that sometimes we're given a whole lot more than we deserve. Thanks, Mom!

"My command is this: Love each other as I have loved you."

John 15:12

CHAPTER 23

Guess Who's Coming to Dinner?

"I had no idea! Why didn't you say something?" I asked my friend on the other end of the telephone line. "How long will she be gone? A week! Well then, why don't you come on over for dinner tonight?" Sue shot a surprised look in my general direction, but it missed, and I continued with my conversation. "Sure, 6:30's fine. We'll see you then. No, don't bring anything, we've got it covered." I hung up the receiver just in time to see a throw pillow hurtling in my direction. Maybe that's how they get the name.

"I don't believe you!" Sue yelled. "How could you do that?"

"How could I do what?" I asked. "I didn't do anything. You threw the pillow at me."

"I'm not talking about the pillow," Sue said.

"Sure, go ahead and change the subject, then."

"I'm not changing the subject." Sue was beginning to appear a bit frustrated. She sometimes frazzles easily in the middle of the simplest conversations. "I'm talking about you inviting John over for dinner tonight."

"Oh, that. No big deal," I explained. "Sheila took the kids to Indiana to visit their grandparents for a week. He's by himself, so I told him to come on over and share dinner with us."

"But you didn't even check with me," Sue said.

"What's the big deal?" I asked. "It's just John. It's not like I invited the king and queen to afternoon tea."

"I don't have anything ready," Sue said, "that's the *big* deal. What am I supposed to feed him?"

"Feed him anything; he's not picky. What were you going to feed us?"

"I was planning on ordering take-out," Sue said.

"So add an order of Kung-pao chicken, and we'll set another place at the table," I said. "Problem solved."

"We can't feed him take-out food," Sue said.

"Why not?"

"Because it's rude to invite someone over for dinner and serve them out of a box, that's why. I wish you would give me a little notice before you invite someone over next time."

Every time I think I have all of the rules figured out, Sue comes up with a new one. I may never master this whole etiquette-and-manners thing.

"Sweetheart, I'm sure take-out food will be fine with John," I said. "It was a spur-of-the-moment invitation. I don't think he's expecting a seven-course meal. He was going to cook for himself, for crying out loud. Can you imagine the gourmet meal he would have whipped up?"

Ignoring me with determination, Sue continued her attempts at salvaging her hostess reputation. "I think there's a tray of lasagna in the freezer," Sue said. "If I defrost it in the microwave, it should be ready to serve by seven."

"I'm sure that will be fine," I agreed, realizing this was one battle I wouldn't win easily.

"It's not fine," Sue countered. "The house is a mess. Why don't you go vacuum the living room while I clean the bathrooms. The kids can wash the dirty dishes."

"Why don't you hide the dirty dishes in the oven, like you do when my discipleship group comes over?" I asked. "That way, the kids can vacuum the living room, and I can watch the basketball game." Sue didn't find this acceptable and made her feelings clear in a manner not suited for retelling in this forum. Besides, she needed the oven to cook the lasagna.

"You invited him," Sue reminded me, "*you* vacuum."

"That's what I was thinking too," I said, heading to the closet to find the upright and its many attachments. "I think I'll do the hall, too, since I have the vacuum out anyway." This was my way of making some minor retribution for my social blunder.

For the next hour, Sue cleaned and defrosted and performed all manner of domestic magic, while I slowly and methodically vacuumed the carpets. I could have finished the job in under fifteen minutes, but I thought it prudent to continue vacuuming until Sue stopped working or called for my assistance elsewhere.

"Would you run to the store and pick up a loaf of Italian bread?" Sue asked. "Italian, not French," she reminded me for good measure.

"That's not really a request, is it?" I asked.

"Not really."

"OK, then. In that case, I'd love to."

By 6:30, the lasagna was warming, the house looked spotless, and a loaf of Italian (not French) bread was sliced, seasoned, and awaiting a turn in the oven. Sue had returned to her normally calm self, and I resumed watching the basketball game while we awaited our friend's arrival. The doorbell rang the moment I settled into my chair.

"Could you get that?" Sue asked. Again, not really a request.

"I'd be glad to," I said, making my way to the door. "By the way, did somebody spill Kool-Aid under the kitchen table?" Sue shot across the room, sponge in hand, sliding the last three feet across the linoleum. "Just kidding, Sweetheart," I said, "but good response time; could be a record." The sponge hit me in the back of the head before I could turn the corner into the front hallway. Out of politeness, I gave Sue an extra second or two to pick up the projectile, so the house would not appear untidy.

"Come on in, John," I said, motioning him through the door. "Excuse the mess, Sue didn't have enough time to paint the house and revarnish all of the baseboards." His laughter distracted him from seeing the scowl Sue wore in my honor. "Let's head on into the living room and catch the end of the game."

"Sure thing," John said, "but where should I put this?" He held out a white box wrapped with string. "It's just some pastries I picked up. I stopped by the bakery on my way over."

"Oh, you didn't have to do that," Sue fawned.

"Yes, he did," I said. "You should of said something, Buddy. I would have had you grab a loaf of Italian bread while you were there." Sue's face contorted again, making me wonder if I had married Lon Chaney or some other master of disguise.

"You two go ahead and watch the game," Sue offered. "Dinner will be ready in no time."

"I hope I'm not putting you out," John said.

"Not at all," Sue answered. "You know you're always welcome here." This time it was my face that contorted, as I led John toward the television. I didn't make it far, though. "Aren't you going to offer John something to drink?" Sue asked.

"He knows where the refrigerator is," I reminded Sue.

"You are impossible," Sue said. "John, can I get you some iced tea or a soda or something."

"No thanks. I'm fine," John answered.

"I could use a glass of tea," I said. I broke the silence that followed by volunteering to get it myself.

John and I caught the last few minutes of the game before Sue called us to the table for dinner. Salad, bread, and lasagna were all well received by our last-minute dinner guest.

"I sure do appreciate you having me over, Sue," John said as she cleared the plates and began serving the pastries.

"Don't give it a second thought," Sue said. "You're not really a guest here, anyway. You're more like family."

"And it was me who invited you, anyway," I reminded.

"Sheila would have had a cow if I invited someone home for dinner without giving her a week's notice," John continued. "She likes to have some time to get the house in order and plan the meal and everything. She really goes off the deep end if I don't give her some advance notice."

"Ah-h-h, Sue's flexible," I said, and smiled at my darling bride. "You don't mind a bit, do you, Sweetheart?"

"Not at all," Sue answered through a very thin smile. "Any time, John."

"As a matter of fact, if you're not doing anything tomorrow night, there's another game on. You're more than welcome to come on over and watch it with me. Potluck, though. I'm not making any promises." Sue's smile grew noticeably thinner.

"I couldn't do that," John said. "I don't want to wear out my welcome." He gave Sue a pleading puppy-dog sort of look that begged her to reflect my invitation.

"Like I said, anytime, John," she responded. "I've got to warn you, though. Tomorrow is Ron's night to cook, so you'll have to risk it." She turned to me with a real smile this time. "You were planning on making Crepes Newburgh and that homemade onion soup, weren't you, Darling?"

"Actually, I planned on ordering take-out," I said, "but I guess crepes sound good too."

"I love crepes," John answered. "I didn't know you were a gourmet cook. Can I bring dessert, or do you bake too?"

"Cream puffs," Sue jumped in. "He likes to bake cream puffs. Don't worry about a thing, we've got it all covered."

"Yeah, covered," I repeated. "We've got it all covered."

I may not know all of the rules, but I can tell when I'm losing the game.

Wisdom has built her house . . . "Let all who are simple come in

here!" she says to those who lack judgment. "Come, eat my food and

drink the wine I have mixed. Leave your simple ways and you will live;

walk in the way of understanding."

Proverbs 9:1a, 4–6

CHAPTER 24

My Immortal Words

"Dad, can I ask you a question?"

"You just did," I pointed out. Staring intently at my computer screen, I was trying to finish a project before the deadline for a change.

"That wasn't it," Ron said. "I have another one." This is the biggest problem with questions: They often come in groups.

"This doesn't have anything to do with your geometry homework, does it?" I asked. "Because if it does, I think I hear your mother calling me."

"Nope, nothing to do with geometry."

"Is money involved? Are you going to ask me to front you some cash for a movie or something?"

"I don't need any money, Dad—unless, of course, you're offering." It's good to know that my son leaves his options open.

"No, I'm not offering," I said. "Just laying the ground rules. How about the car? You aren't going to ask for my car, are you?"

"No, Dad!" Ron said, a degree of frustration in his voice. "Can I just ask the question?"

"Go ahead, shoot," I said. "You know I'm always available for you."

"What do you want your tombstone to read?" Ron asked.

"I beg your pardon?" I wasn't sure I heard him correctly.

"You know, like an inscription," he explained. "What would you like to have carved on your tombstone?"

"The future resting place of Ron Darbee, Sr.," I offered, "seeing as how I'm not planning on needing a grave marker any time soon. And from now on, just act like a normal teenager and ask me for money, will you? I hope this isn't about me grounding you last weekend. You aren't holding a grudge or anything, are you?"

"It's a homework assignment, Dad."

"What ever happened to 'What I did on my summer vacation' papers? What kind of a class is this, anyway?"

"Sociology. We're talking about how people perceive themselves and how they want to be remembered."

"Kind of a morbid way of going about it, if you ask me," I said. "Who's teaching this class, Stephen King?"

"Come on, Dad, this is serious. If you were dead, what would you like on your tombstone?"

"Ron, if I were dead, I don't think I would care."

"Fine, if you won't help, I'll just make something up," Ron threatened. "How does this sound? 'Here lies Ron Darbee, Sr.

He smelled so bad we had to bury him.' Or how about this? 'He gave his life to liberal causes.'"

"Funny," I said. "Very funny. Do you know what yours is going to say?"

"No, what?"

"His sarcasm cost him a college education."

"I don't get it, Dad."

"That's right," I said, "and if you keep this up, you never will."

Death isn't a topic I spend much time dwelling on, so I didn't have a good answer for my son. But since it was a homework assignment, and I insist that the kids take their homework seriously, I offered to think about the question and get back with him. "When is this due?" I asked.

"Next week."

"OK, then let me mull this around, and I'll have something appropriate when I get home tomorrow afternoon."

As promised, I gave Ron's question some serious consideration, yet I still came to the same conclusion: once I'm gone, it doesn't matter much what my tombstone says. Aside from the occasional gardener and a few close relatives, I doubt the thing will be widely read, and I won't be there to receive the criticism at any rate. Still, a writer is probably expected to come up with something more than his dates of birth and death, and I felt like I owed Ron a reasonable attempt. As I do with most questions that stump me, I sought my wife's opinion.

"Did Ron talk to you about his homework assignment?" I asked Sue as we prepared for bed that evening.

"Yeah, why?" she asked.

"Because he ran the assignment by me, and I drew a complete blank," I said. "What did you tell him?"

"$A^2 + B^2 = C^2$," Sue said. "It's the Pythagorean theorem. He learned it in algebra last year. You should know that."

It didn't take me long to realize that we were talking about two completely different questions. Either that, or Sue wanted a tombstone shaped like a perfect right triangle.

"That's not the question I was talking about," I said. "He asked me to come up with my own epitaph."

"Why?" Sue asked, and I filled her in on the details.

"That seems easy enough," Sue said. "You should be able to come up with something reasonable."

"Oh really? And I suppose you already know what you want your monument to read?" I asked.

"Loving mother and faithful wife," Sue answered.

"That's pathetic."

"What's wrong with that?" Sue asked.

"Nothing's wrong with the words, Sue. But it's a little eerie knowing you have this all figured out ahead of time. You haven't bought adjoining plots that I'm not aware of, have you?"

"I thought we'd be buried in my family's plot in Minnesota."

"Not me," I said. "You know I can't stand the cold."

The subject of death doesn't come up much in pleasant conversation, and I suppose I can understand why. It's usually associated with sadness or the loss of a loved one, and it reminds us of our own mortality. Kind of hard to work that in at parties. Even Christians, men and women who trust the promises of eternal life through faith in Jesus Christ, often avoid the subject altogether. Maybe it's because we don't think God is quite through with us here, or possibly we still cling to a small amount of fear. Likely, it is both and more.

I can honestly say that I believe the promises of God with

all of my heart and soul. With that on record, I'll also say that where passing from this life is concerned, I'm not trying to hurry the process along any. God will take me in his own good time, and I don't intend to rush him, regardless of what Dr. Kevorkian might say.

All things considered, I viewed Ron's sociology question from a new perspective. His teacher wasn't asking simply what I wanted my marker to say, but what I hoped my life would say about me. What would I leave behind? What would be my legacy? That shed some light on the issue. What did my life say about me? I started to draft my epitaph.

"Loving father and faithful husband" came the first attempt. I threw that one away for fear Sue might claim plagiarism.

"Faithful father and loving husband" went the same route.

"Adequate husband and father" sounded kind of weak, and "dutiful son" might prove tough to substantiate—something a guy doesn't want to worry about when he's planning to meet his Maker.

"Hey, Sue," I asked, "how does 'he still had most of his own hair' sound to you?"

"Dumb, but optimistic," was her supportive response.

I made a list of all the positive qualities that came to mind and started marking those off that seemed inappropriate. Faithful servant—I'd sure like to take that one, but to be honest, my life would benefit from less television and more service—gone. I crossed out "stalwart evangelist" before I finished writing it on the pad. "Studious disciple" came close, but "cyclic disciple" was more accurate and far less complimentary. Neither teacher nor leader fit, nor did missionary, minister, or mentor. All of these qualities were part of my life at one time or another. Some I did well, others I did not, but none of them truly defines who I am. I found myself at a loss for words.

I allowed myself a night to sleep on the subject, and over coffee the next morning penned my hopefully far from final words. Certainly there are more eloquent epitaphs, but I'd like to think few convey a message with more accuracy. I waited for Ron at the breakfast table, anxious to share the results of my effort.

"I had some time to think about your question last night," I said while Ron poured a bowl of cereal. "I think I've come up with an answer."

"That's OK, Dad. I've got it: $A^2 + B^2 = C^2$. Mom already reminded me. I can't believe I forgot that."

"Not that question, Ron. The other one. The one about my tombstone."

"Oh yeah, that. It's not due until next week."

"Well, I don't need another week," I said. "I'm ready right now."

"Can you write it down and stick it in my backpack, then?" he asked, "because I'll forget it otherwise."

"No, I won't stick it in your backpack. This is the defining statement of my life we're talking about. You're gonna sit there and listen to every word of it."

"Do I have to?" Ron asked.

"You know, you get a step closer to slinging burgers for a living every day," I reminded. "You better start praying for a scholarship right now."

"OK, OK, I'll listen." He couldn't wait to hear what I came up with.

"Here goes: 'He followed the path of God, often walking, occasionally running, and sometimes being dragged along.' That's it," I said. "That's me. I love God and want to live my life according to his will, but I struggle from time to time. Sometimes I walk along with the body, other times I'm out front leading, and once in a while I'm reluctant or selfish, but God still pulls me along for my own good. What do you think?"

"I think you need a hobby," Ron said. "Looks like you spent more time on this assignment than I did."

"You don't like it?"

"No, it's fine. I just expected something simple, like 'Rest in peace' or something funny, like, 'I'd rather be in Philadelphia.' But this is OK, too, I guess."

"All of these threats about college money don't mean anything to you, do they, Ron?"

"Nope, not really."

"Why not?" I asked. "Will you please answer me that?"

"Because if I don't go to college, I'll have to live with you until I can afford my own place. I figure you'll foot the bill."

"I figure you're right," I said, "but who's going to help you with your sociology homework?"

"I can always ask Mom, if you'd rather handle the math, Dad."

I'm still looking for my college textbooks. I need to brush up a bit.

In the way of righteousness there is life; along that path is immortality.

Proverbs 12:28

CHAPTER 25

She Loves Me, She Loves Me Not

"Hey, that's her," Tony said, motioning toward a girl riding a bicycle down our block. She had long, jet-black hair and large, beautiful, brown eyes.

"Yeah, that's her, all right," someone responded. "Man, she sure is pretty, isn't she?" A chorus of agreements rose up from most of the guys.

I didn't offer an opinion or add my agreement to those stated, feeling it would be inappropriate for me to respond.

The poor girl was absolutely enamored with me, and I could hardly blame her. With all of my boyish charm and my suave, sophisticated manner, I expected to draw her attention. Of course, she tried to hide the attraction by pretending to forget my name and making believe I didn't exist, but I saw right through her thin facade. The signs were all there, and she was sending out signals like a third-base coach with runners on. Her name was Teresa DeCarlo, the prettiest girl in the fourth grade, except maybe for Stephanie Galante, who belonged in the seventh grade and, therefore, was disqualified from our age bracket. I thought about letting Teresa know I shared her feelings, but I chose to hold back and play hard to get.

Each day in Mr. Taylor's class, I stared intently into her left ear from my desk next to hers, while her eyes remained fixed on the blackboard. She never turned in my direction, not even when I dropped a book or pretended to bludgeon myself with a stapler. Even when I performed my famous walrus impression, sticking pencils in my nose and swallowing goldfish crackers whole, she never initiated eye contact. Her unnatural attempts to appear disinterested convinced me of her infatuation, and my heart almost broke watching her suffer in lonely silence.

One afternoon, my friends and I walked past her on our way home from school, and it was all she could do to control her passions. Rather than ignoring me, her usual ploy, she stuck a finger down her throat and pretended to vomit. Her friends laughed along with her, just for show, but they must have known too. I felt sorry for the poor creature, wearing her emotions on her sleeve as she was, and decided that leaving her hanging by a thread any longer would be cruel and heartless. I began planning my first move.

An honest and forthright declaration of my feelings was out of the question. To do so would have violated the solemn code that preadolescent boys live by, namely, never admit you like a girl unless she first makes public her feelings for you. Not only does this code protect boys from the pains of rejection, it also serves as training for manhood, where we will suppress even stronger emotions from wives and other loved ones and strive to become the best basket cases we can be. No, there had to be another way.

Many of my peers favored the 'pass it on' approach to first contact with the feminine gender. In this scenario, the potential Romeo casually mentions to a close friend that he might not find the fair Juliet utterly disgusting, and asks him to ferret out her true feelings. Romeo's friend passes the information on to another friend, saying, "Romeo might like Juliet, but he wants to know if Juliet likes him back." This information progresses through a succession of seventeen or eighteen friends before reaching the intended, who responds by saying something like "Maybe, but find out if he likes me first." The chain is then reactivated in reverse for several iterations until a declaration of their mutual feelings for each other is announced at their ten-year high school reunion. I ruled this option out, doubting Teresa could hold up that long.

Knowing that actions speak louder than words, I decided to express my feelings in the form of my deeds. That way Teresa would know exactly how I felt and feel free to vocalize her affections. I started with a gentle yank on her ponytail in the middle of our math lesson, an act that finally gave the girl enough courage to make eye contact. She yelled and complained to the teacher in order to hide her true feelings, and I spent the remainder of the day with my nose in a corner, but, overall, the endeavor was an unqualified success. I stepped up my efforts another notch.

On the playground, I pelted Teresa with rubber balls and ran right through the middle of her hopscotch game. I hid her books in the coat closet during class and made disgusting noises while she ate lunch. Not a day went by without me jumping out of a bush or from behind a car to scare the living daylights out of her on the trip to or from school. I gave her every opportunity, yet shyness prevailed.

Not one to be discouraged easily when true love beckons, I began calling her childish names and making up clever rhymes about her lineage. She continued to appear distant and aloof to the casual observer, but I could tell my actions were wearing her down. She started doodling my name on her book covers and drawing caricatures of me in class. "Teresa hates Ron" adorned several textbooks, accompanied by a stick figure with a pig's head and my trademark baseball cap. While I was obviously flattered by her attempts to immortalize my image through artistic expression, she appeared to be taking this thing more seriously than I realized. We were far too young for a relationship of this magnitude, and I deemed it best to put an end to the romance before Teresa started making wedding plans and picking out drapes. Always the gentleman, I vowed to let her down easy.

The next morning, I gently tapped her on the shoulder during the morning announcements. She turned toward me with devotion in her eyes and stuck out her tongue in a display of undying love and admiration. This wasn't going to be easy for the poor girl.

"You know I don't like you," I whispered.

Finding it difficult to keep her eyes off of me, she turned again and whispered, "I don't like you either."

"Yeah, well, I don't like you even more than you don't like me," I responded.

Sensing that what we once shared was coming to an end, Teresa tried her best to cling to some remnant of our life together. "I don't like you a million times more than you don't like me," she said. Though I knew we had to end this reckless affair of ours, it hurt me to see her strike out in desperation like that. I could have easily come back with something witty like, "I don't like you infinity times more than you don't like me," but I realized it was better to let her have the last word. She needed the closure.

Nothing more ever came of our brief romance, and the remainder of our school years passed without either of us bringing the subject up. We had different friends and traveled in different circles; it was easier to avoid speaking to each other than risk dredging up old feelings. I've got the memory of my first love locked away in a small corner of my mind. It will always be special, always the first.

Many years later, when I proposed to Sue, I thought it only fair to clear the air and let her know about the special relationship Teresa and I shared. A marriage should start with a clean slate, no secrets, no hidden past. I filled her in on every detail, and I must admit she took it remarkably well. There was an outbreak of hysterical laughter as she attempted to hide the pain my admission caused, but to her credit, she never broached the subject again. As far as Sue is concerned, my relationship with Teresa never existed.

I am so thankful for a wife who looks at life in such a mature and adult fashion. Rather than dwell on our past, she concentrates on our future. There's not a jealous bone in her body—well, maybe one.

"If it's a boy, I'd like to name him Robert," I said when we were expecting our second child. "And if it's a girl, maybe Teresa."

"Robert's good," Sue said, "but I think I like Melissa better for a girl."

"How come?" I asked, already knowing the answer.

"I don't know, it's just a pretty name."

I let the unflattering bout of jealousy pass unnoticed. After all, I could hardly blame her.

There is no fear in love. But perfect love drives out fear, because fear has to do with punishment. The one who fears is not made perfect in love. We love because he first loved us.

1 John 4:18–19

CHAPTER 26

Will My Real Father Please Step Forward?

After more than forty years of dedicated service to the same organization, I figured he deserved to retire. At the age of fifty-eight, my father accepted an offer for early retirement and left the company he joined shortly after turning seventeen. Mom and Dad managed their finances intelligently over the years, and while they certainly weren't poised to live extravagantly, they were prepared to live in what they termed as "cautious comfort." We threw Dad a party; we wished him well; we hoped he would enjoy a well-deserved period of rest and relaxation. What we didn't expect was massive change.

My dad, the man I always pictured with a suit and tie, has transformed into something totally different—part Bob Villa, part Julia Childs, with just enough Grizzly Adams mixed in to make him a threat to our national forests. I've got to say, the man scares me to death. Within weeks of leaving the business world, Dad stopped quoting Lee Iacocca and started referencing Kathy Lee. After two years, he now views Regis Philbin as a visionary and Graham Kerr as a mentor. He plans to join Oprah's book club just as soon as he perfects his soufflé, but he won't find time for that until he builds a new deck in the backyard from trees he fells, planks, and finishes by hand. Any worries I had about Dad growing bored have passed. Now I just hope he doesn't run off and join the circus.

"Don't slam the door," Dad yelled the last time I went home for a visit. "I've got a cake in the oven." OK, so maybe I let the door close a little harder than necessary, but I didn't want anyone to see him in his attire of the moment.

"You're baking?" I asked. "Well, isn't that special. I think you and I need to sit down and talk."

"What? Baking isn't masculine enough for your old man? I'll show you what's masculine." He assumed the crab posture for my entertainment—bending slightly forward at the waist and extending his arms out in a near complete circle while flexing his entire upper body. You haven't experienced true nausea until you've witnessed a sixty-year-old grandfather performing muscle-man poses in a lace-fringed apron. Take my word for it; it's not a pretty sight.

"I've still got it," he boasted.

"Yeah, and when you get it diagnosed, let me know what it is," I requested. "And please tell me you're wearing something underneath that apron."

"Shorts." He hoisted the hem to reveal knee-length plaid shorts, a bold and daring fashion statement.

"Dad, what happened to that barbecue apron I bought you that said 'King of the Grill' across the chest?" I asked. "Couldn't you at least wear that?"

"Not enough pockets. I like to keep my tools handy." He

demonstrated the versatility of his garment by pulling a whisk, wooden spoon, and oven thermometer from the pockets at his waist like so many rabbits from a magician's hat.

"At least, ask Mom to iron on a picture of Michael Jordan or a race car or something, will you? And stop calling them 'your tools'; they're utensils. You're giving me the creeps here, Dad."

"So I guess you won't be having any cake, then."

"No, that would be rude of me," I explained. "I'll eat some cake, but only to be supportive. Speaking of support, would you mind throwing a T-shirt on under that apron?"

"I'm gonna throw you in a minute," he threatened. To be honest, I believe he still could. That ought to give you an idea of the domestic side of my father that has emerged, but there are other sides as well.

Dad has always considered himself a country boy, by rite of his birth in the rural Catskill Mountains. The fact that he moved to Long Island at the age of eight did little to change his self-image. It's sort of a taking the boy out of the country, but not the country out of the boy kind of thing. Now that he has all of this time on his hands and a few resources at his disposal, what I call the "Grizzly Adams Complex" has begun to set in.

In planning for their retirement, my parents purchased a second home in Dad's native Catskills. They refer to it as a "cabin," but aside from the natural wood siding, relative seclusion, and the wooded acreage surrounding, I doubt it fits even the loosest definition of the word. Cabins, to the best of my knowledge, are somewhat smaller than sixteen hundred square feet, and few include finished basements. Abe Lincoln lived in a real cabin; Honest Abe didn't own a satellite dish. Andrew Jackson lived in a cabin; Andrew Jackson carried his water indoors. I'm willing to bet neither of them ever saw pulsating jets in their hot tubs unless they bathed with a straw, and their only skylights were an indication that the roof needed repair. They lived in real, honest-to-goodness, down-home American cabins. My parents just own a house that's hard to find. But we'll call it a cabin, because it makes Dad feel better.

Of course, a great outdoorsman like my father couldn't survive in the wilderness without a few essentials. A hydraulic log splitter tops his list of purchases, followed closely by a wood chipper capable of reducing titanium alloys to their individual atomic particles. The chain saw he brought home would send Paul Bunyan and his blue ox, Babe, crying all the way back to the toothpick factory from whence they came. That he owns these toys disturbs me; that he attempts to operate them without adult supervision sends chills up and down my spine. I'm afraid he's going to hurt himself, if the animals don't get to him first.

We'll call this new side of my father the "Eule Gibbons/Doctor Doolittle Syndrome." One hundred and forty-eight varieties of edible shrubs, nuts, ferns, bark, mushrooms, and grass adorn my father's property, or so I'm told. If you happen to wander by, he'll make you a stew with these ingredients, and he'll make you eat it too. I think he ate a bad mushroom somewhere down the line. He's also communing with God's furry creatures on a dangerous scale. It wouldn't be so bad if he was satisfied with talking to the animals, but he insists on comparing paw sizes.

Mom and Dad put out a salt lick, hoping to attract deer from the surrounding forest. The plan worked so remarkably well that they began purchasing corn in wholesale lots to feed the does and fawns to keep them coming to their doorstep year round. This turned out to be one of your classic "good initiative, poor judgment" kind of plans, however, as they found out when a rather large, hungry (and did I say large?) black bear decided to invite himself/herself—I didn't perform a thorough examination—to the feast. Maybe you know how to dissuade a hungry bear from eating the deer's corn, but I assure you, I do not. As it turned out, neither did my father.

When efforts to scare the bear away failed—my father went out in the yard in his apron; the bear appeared shocked, but certainly not frightened—my father cut off his, and the deer's, food supply. The deer left in a most orderly and cooperative manner. The bear, on the other hand, proved somewhat more stubborn.

Yogi decided that if the food supply on the outside had dried up, certainly he would be welcome to dine on the inside of the house with our family. Apparently, the bear had been training on a Stairmaster, because he handled the flight up to the front deck like Rocky Balboa in front of the Philadelphia courthouse. Rising up on his hind legs, Yogi put his front paws against the sliding glass doors and peered inside—I assume, either looking for food or trying to identify the shrill, high-pitched screaming emanating from somewhere in the vicinity of my mother. Always curious, Dad used this rare Kodak moment to further his studies of bear anatomy. Placing his hands against the glass, he stood face-to-face with Yogi and compared paw sizes. Dad was thrilled, Mom terrified, and I was just simply amazed.

"Are you out of your mind?" I yelled at him later. Much later actually, after I shaved, showered, and found myself a clean pair of underwear.

"Oh, don't make such a big deal out of this," my father argued. "It's just a bear. He's not gonna hurt us."

"It's a bear, Dad! A *bear*! He could have killed you if he had the mind to."

"He was on the other side of the sliding glass door," my father pointed out. "That's double-pane glass you know. No way is he coming through there." I find it difficult to argue with logic like that.

The most recent side of my father to emerge we call his "Sears Craftsman Period." Not only is he intent on building the better mousetrap, but also I believe he has begun construction on a small suspension bridge in the backyard. While there are some power tools involved, so far he hasn't hurt anything. To date, Dad has built a few dozen lawn silhouettes for the neighbors, the red wagon he promised me when I was six, and a hand-carved oak toilet seat. Three months ago, he decided to branch out and enrolled in a stained-glass class at the local adult education center.

"What is this, Dad?" I asked, examining a drawing I found on his kitchen table.

"Oh, that. That's my rose window. I'm going to make it when I finish this class."

"I think you screwed up the dimensions, Dad. It says here the diameter is six feet."

"Nope, six feet should be about right," he said. "I want to surprise your mother with it and install it on the front of the house. She always wanted a rose window."

"Are you kidding me?" I asked. "Dad, this is too big!"

"I've seen lots of them that size," he argued.

"Where? Notre Dame? You planning on throwing in a few flying buttresses while you're at it?"

"Too gothic," he said. "Think I'll just stick with a rose window."

Now that I've finally resolved myself to my father's many

new sides, another, more familiar side is emerging—the one with the suit and tie. He received a phone call the other day from his former employer. It seems they miss him and would like Dad to fill a void. They offered to bring him back to work on a consulting basis—four days a week.

"That's great news, Dad!" I shouted when I heard about the offer. "When do you start?"

"I'm not sure I'm ready to go back to work," my father said. "I have so many projects going, I can't just get up and walk away from them. The extra money would be nice, but it means taking the train into Manhattan again. I'm not sure I'm ready for that."

"Please promise me you'll give it some serious thought," I begged. At least with Manhattan, I understand the risks.

"Listen to me, O house of Jacob, all you who remain of the house of Israel, you whom I have upheld since you were conceived, and have carried since your birth. Even to your old age and gray hairs I am he, I am he who will sustain you. I have made you and I will carry you; I will sustain you and I will rescue you."

Isaiah 46:3–4

CHAPTER 21

The Best Laid Plans

"When I grow up, I want to be . . ." The words are filled with hope and promise, infused with aspiration, the fuel of childish dreams: "When I grow up, I want to be president." "When I grow up, I want to play pro ball." "When I grow up, I want to walk on the moon." And when we are six or seven, maybe even as old as eighteen, our "I want to be" potential seems limitless. Every dream looms only a few short steps beyond reality. Achieving our goals appears a minor battle, conquerable once we strike out on our own.

"What do you want to be when you grow up?" I threw the question out to no one in particular one summer afternoon as my friends and I lounged casually on the sidewalk in front of Anthony Gianelli's home. A considerate neighbor had charitably "adjusted" a fire hydrant, and we were resting in the cool stream flowing downhill toward the next sewer grate. Our energy already spent in the effort of running back and forth in front of the source, we were content to let the smaller kids play while we caught our breath.

"I want to be a doctor," Elliot Pelzman proclaimed, "like my Uncle Benjamin." Considering Elliot's grades in school, we saw the medical field as well within his grasp.

"I want to be a lawyer," said my friend Mickey.

"I want to drive my own race car," was Artie's plan for the future.

We also had an aspiring astronaut in our group, a future high-powered businessman, and more than one fireman. My own dream of playing second base for the New York Yankees was well known, though not necessarily considered a likely possibility. But of all the "I want to be's" stated, Tony, our host for the afternoon, provided us with the greatest surprise.

"I'm gonna be a cop when I grow up," Tony announced; which brought laughter from all assembled and put Tony immediately on the defensive. "What's the matter with that?" he asked. "There's nothin' wrong with bein' a cop."

Obviously, we didn't see anything wrong with joining the police force, and several boys shouted their concurrence, agreeing that a career in law enforcement was certainly a goal worthy of pursuit. The laughter, Elliot felt compelled to explain, was directed not at the choice of employment but toward the young man who considered himself a prospective employee.

"You can't be a cop," Elliot said.

"Why not?"

"Because you're already a hoodlum. That's why not."

"I'm not a hoodlum," Tony argued. "I just get in trouble sometimes." Sometimes was defined as whenever the opportunity presented itself. We all pictured Tony's future with a strong tie to crime, but leaning more to the side of advocate than adversary. Of all the guys in our close-knit circle, Anthony Gianelli was seen as the most likely recipient of an all-expenses paid trip to a juvenile detention center. I figured I stood a better chance of donning the Yankee pinstripes than Tony did of wearing a badge on a shirt of New York blue.

"What's the angle, Tony?" Artie asked. "Figure you can get first dibs on the really good robberies if you get an inside line?"

"Maybe he thinks the police department will offer him a job, just so they ain't gotta chase him around anymore," Mickey offered. This prompted another raucous response from the crowd, and everyone shared in the laughter, with one noted exception.

"Cops carry handcuffs, they don't wear 'em" was shouted from someone in the group, followed by: "Tony G. The first Gianelli on the right side of the bars," a remark immediately recognized as having gone too far. Tony shot up from the sidewalk and glared menacingly at each of us in turn and, for once, found himself at a loss for words. Obviously angry, and probably hurt, Tony stomped up the steps and through his front doorway, apparently intent on parting company. His grandmother held a conflicting viewpoint, however, regarding where, at that moment, Tony belonged.

"Get outta my house with your nasty, wet body!" we heard shouted through the open window. "What's amatta with you! You don't see the clean floor? I don't work hard enough, you wanna see me mop it again?"

"But, Grandma, I wanna come in!" we heard Tony whine.

"And I wanna look like Sophia Loren, but you don't see any cameras out front, do you? Now get outta this house and dry off!" A smattering of Italian laced the conversation, but as I'm not sure of the spelling or entirely comfortable with the appropriateness of the translation, I'll edit that part out. The result, anyway, was the reappearance of a dejected Tony in our midst.

"Come on over and sit down," I called to our forlorn friend. "Nobody meant anything serious. We were just having a little fun." Tony chose to brood in silence a few minutes longer, however, and as I guess we felt somewhat responsible for his sudden shift in mood, we kept pretty quiet ourselves.

For children, staying quiet even for a few brief minutes feels like an eternity, and when it appeared that eternity might never end, Elliot broke our silence, "I guess Tony could be a cop if he wanted to."

"What are you, nuts?" Artie challenged. The looks of disapproval his comment solicited from our group prompted a quick, if not heartfelt rebuttal. "Oh, yeah, I guess he could be a cop if he really wanted to," Artie corrected himself. Only a few of us heard "And I could be the queen of England" that he mumbled beneath his breath.

Seeing this as an opportunity to gain a degree of affirmation for myself, I joined in with, "And I could play for the Yanks if I really wanted to."

"Maybe you could be a cop, too," Mickey suggested, and though I knew he meant well, I didn't find his comment at all uplifting.

"You wait and see," Tony said, ending his self-imposed period of exile. "I'll show you. Someday I'm gonna be a cop." Each and every one of us nodded our agreement.

After all these years, I still keep in touch with most of

those guys, and on the rare occasions when two or three of us find ourselves in the same state, we get together for dinner or just to discuss old times. It's funny to see how much we have grown from the wide-eyed wonder of our youth, and how quickly the plans we made were forgotten.

I would love to end this story by telling you that Anthony Gianelli went on to the police academy and joined the forces of good to battle crime and ensure the safety of New York's streets. The truth is, he sells security doors for a company in Queens, which I suppose is still law enforcement if you look at it with a liberal eye. On a promising note, Tony didn't turn out to be the hoodlum his youthful actions foreshadowed, and he makes an honest living if you don't consider the markup on those security doors.

If Elliot does any doctoring, it would be to the books he keeps for a shipping firm out of Staten Island. He did start his college education as a premed student, but changed his major to accounting when he realized he couldn't handle the sight of blood. Rumor has it that my old friend couldn't cut a rare steak without feeling light-headed, so we're all better off for the change.

Mickey isn't a lawyer, but he did represent himself in small claims court after someone ran a red light and torpedoed the side of his minivan. Artie works as a network analyst for a computer software company.

No one hailing from our neighborhood works for NASA, and I don't think we produced any firemen, but none of that really matters anymore. The childish dreams that seemed so important and the plans we made in our youth gave way to adult responsibilities and expectations. If you measured success by the goals of our boyhood, each of us failed miserably; but, thankfully, no one holds us to that standard. If we failed at anything, it was in failing to remember that God has his own plans for our lives, and his plans don't always line up with ours.

Oh, yeah, and me. I'm still waiting for George Steinbrenner's call announcing my debut at Yankee Stadium. My mitt's all oiled up, and my cleats are clean. I'm ready to go at a moment's notice. So far, the phone isn't ringing off the hook, but it's probably just a negotiating ploy. You know how George is about salaries. In the meantime, I'll continue to live and serve where God places me. I just hope that it's not with the Phillies. I had my heart set on the American League.

Now listen, you who say, "Today or tomorrow we will go to this or that city, spend a year there, carry on business and make money." Why, you do not even know what will happen tomorrow. What is your life? You are a mist that appears for a little while and then vanishes. Instead, you ought to say, "If it is the Lord's will, we will live and do this or that."

James 4:13–15

CHAPTER 20

Home Is Where the Refrigerator Is

Every now and then, I pull out the previous year's tax return and read over the names I listed as deductions. We have a total of four, including myself, and I think the system is shortchanging me somehow. When I make a count, I come up with considerably more than four people running around my house and sucking down my food. I'm sure if I found the right accountant, we could find a legal way of reducing this family's tax burden.

Sue and I knew going into this parenting business that we would be required to raise our children. On some level, I even suppose we figured on providing food, clothing, and other staples of life. Braces came as a surprise, but only because we hadn't thought far enough ahead. What we didn't budget for were the extras that keep showing up in our home movies — call them the supporting cast, if you will, or the cast I am supporting. Their numbers are growing, lately, at an almost exponential rate.

I tell you with all honesty that we in no way fit the definition of "cool parents." We don't give our kids' friends free reign of our home, nor do we invite stragglers to set up residence. I don't even go out of my way to be nice to them, yet for some reason they keep coming back. Apparently, they think I'm joking when I point them toward the front door and bid them never to return again. I'm going to need to work on my delivery.

"And who might you be?" I said to the unfamiliar jeans and high tops attached to the young man rummaging in our refrigerator. Returning home from a day at work, this was the first sight that greeted me, and I felt an introduction was in order.

"I'm Ron's friend," came from the vicinity of the crisper drawer, so I knew there was a head in there somewhere.

"Now that's an interesting name," I said. "You must have very creative parents. Tell me, Ron's friend, have you seen Ron around here lately?"

"I think he's in the living room," the voice answered. "Who are you?" A question that gave me insight into the boy's power of deductive reasoning.

"I'm the guy who stocks the refrigerator," I said. "But don't let me rush you. I can wait until you finish taking inventory."

"Cool, is that like a job?"

"I like to think of it as a calling," I answered. "My real job doesn't offer me near the opportunities to interact with interesting people like yourself. By the way, did you know that recent studies show that long-term exposure to refrigerator light kills brain cells?"

"No way. That's cool," the vagrant answered.

"Never mind," I said. "The damage is already done." I walked off in search of the vagrant's host.

"Hi, Dad," Ron greeted from in front of the television. "I didn't know you were home."

"Oh, yeah. I'm home," I said. "Ron, can you tell me who belongs to the blue jeans poking out of my refrigerator?"

"That's Robert. He came over to watch *Deep Space Nine*, then we're going to the comic store."

"Doesn't he have a refrigerator of his own?" I asked.

"I don't think so, but his parents probably do," Ron answered in that honor-student way he has of answering my inquiries. "Why do you ask?"

"Never mind. It doesn't matter," I said. Sarcasm loses its edge if you need to explain it.

Even though I complain from time to time, there is some comfort associated with having all of these kids hanging around. I always know where my own kids are, and at least this way, any fears I have about who they're hanging around with are based on firsthand knowledge. It's the stragglers who are beginning to feel at home here that cause me the most concern.

"Hi, Dad," someone said from behind me. While the voice was familiar, it wasn't familiar enough to belong to someone I own a birth certificate for.

"What did you call me?" I asked my son's friend, James.

"Dad. I figured I'm spending enough time here, I might as well call you Dad too."

"Well, isn't that nice. I'm touched, really," I said. "Don't ever do that again." The boy laughed, apparently finding my comment humorous, so I tried a different approach. "Actually, you're welcome to call me whatever you want, but I'm going to add your name to the chore list the next time you call me Dad."

"Will I get paid?"

"Yeah, but I don't think you'll like the wages," I said. "I've received a number of complaints from my current employees."

"Be glad you're not part of this family," Ron added. "The gene pool is polluted. I figure I'm pretty much doomed."

"In any case, James," I continued, for the moment ignoring Ron's slam, "I think I speak for both Mrs. Darbee and myself when I say we don't plan to help you with college."

"That's OK," James said. "My real parents will take care of that."

"You're already making me proud, son," I said, and patted the boy on the back. "Now take out the garbage." He did, too, and without being told a second time, which is more than I'll say for his brother, my natural son.

"Can James eat here?" Ron asked, stepping out of the way to let his friend get by with the garbage.

"Looks to me like he's already eating here," I said, motioning to a raw hot dog protruding from the kid's mouth, "unless that's a really cheap cigar, in which case we need to have another discussion."

"That's just a snack," Ron said. "Can he eat dinner with us?"

"I suppose," I said, "but check with your mom and make sure she made enough gruel for everybody."

"What's gruel?" James asked.

"Let it go," Ron suggested. "It has to do with that gene-pool thing I mentioned earlier."

So for now, we are resigned to entertaining an extended family, even if the IRS won't let us claim them on our taxes. Even with all of the raids on our refrigerator and sleeping bags on the living room floor, I'm glad our kids feel comfortable enough to invite their friends into this home. Who knows, maybe this is the year Congress passes a partial dependency act and I get to take advantage of a little tax relief.

"Who's this?" I asked Melissa as she walked past my station at the computer and headed for her room.

"Oh, this is my new friend, Samantha," Melissa said. "Her family just moved here."

"Hello, Samantha. I'm Mr. Darbee, Melissa's father. Say, your dad doesn't happen to be a congressman, does he?"

"No, he's an electrician," she answered, "but he votes."

Melissa, fearing I might say something to embarrass her, pulled Samantha from the room before I had a chance to get to know her very well. No matter, she'll be back soon enough. They always are.

Do not forsake your friend and the friend of your father, and do not go to your brother's house when disaster strikes you — better a neighbor nearby than a brother far away.

Proverbs 27:10

CHAPTER 29

The Answer Is Blowing in the Wind

I've spent a lot of time trying to get my life organized, planning for this or that eventuality, plotting out the various sequences of events. So why is it that every time I get all of my ducks in a row, somebody comes and moves one of my ducks? I'm a nice enough guy. I try to live by the philosophy that I don't mess with your ducks, you don't mess with mine, and everyone remains happy. But life doesn't work that way.

Or maybe everyone else comes together in some grand consensus and decides that ducks are no longer important or that ducks shouldn't be in rows at all. They might even claim that my ducks are polluting the environment and stick me with a bill to clean up the nasty duck mess. Suddenly all of the planning—all of the organization—is for naught, and I find myself right back at the beginning—ready to start the entire process all over again, but this time without the ducks.

Just take a couple of deep breaths. All right, I'm better now.

OK, so I'm not really talking about ducks. I'm talking about change, the kind of change that throws a monkey wrench into the gears of planning and yanks us right out of our comfort zones. Change is one of the few constants in life and usually comes when we least expect it. Not that I'm against change, per se. For once, I just want to be the guy instituting the change, the guy in control of the variables, the guy with some vision of how the change will effect my life. Is that asking too much?

Our church home recently underwent some major changes that involved staff moving on and the reevaluation of many ministries. At first, I handled things pretty well. I told myself it didn't matter. I told myself and anyone who would listen that God is in control, and whoever God meant to lead our church would surface. I was pretty proud of myself. But after waiting the requisite two or three weeks with no sign of permanence or stability on the horizon, I slipped back into old ways and began to worry.

Sometimes I think that worry is underrated in terms of value and productivity. My worry quickly paid dividends, growing first into concern before shooting up the charts into full-blown dissatisfaction. At some point, I decided to share this dissatisfaction with a close friend who also happens to be a pastor. We scheduled a lunch.

Over a bowl of noodles at a local Chinese restaurant, he listened to my entire story. I started by explaining the little worries, moved into the concerns, and for the grand finale unloaded the dissatisfaction. To ensure that I effectively conveyed the entire range of emotions, I even shared the duck analogy, hoping it would clarify my major points. It didn't help.

"Change is like a tree in the wind," my friend told me. "If you remain flexible and bend, you will either adapt or it will pass. But if you remain rigid and unmoving, chances are pretty good you're going to break. The wind is going to come, so you might as well learn to deal with it."

"What are you talking about?" I asked.

"Change," he answered. "You told me how you felt about some of the changes, and now I'm trying to explain it to you."

"So what's with the wind?" I asked. "One minute I'm telling you about ducks, and the next minute you're reliving some old Bob Dylan song, and 'the answer is blowing in the wind.' I hope you don't do a lot of counseling."

"Eat your noodles," he said.

Why is it that when we know we have all of the answers, nobody wants to listen? I had thought long and hard about these concerns of mine, and in so doing, I determined all of the problems and was prepared to offer all of the solutions. I didn't want advice about how to accept change. I wanted the change to go away. I saw a problem, and I was ready to fix it. That's who I am; that's how I'm wired.

And then I heard it. In the back of my mind, from a time long ago, it rose above the worries and concerns: I think I can, I think I can. *I think I just did*, I told myself. Once again, I allowed common sense and self-reliance to take the place reserved for trust. Rather than faithfully putting my concerns in God's hands, I wanted to fix the problem my own way and on my own schedule. It didn't work; it never does.

Like the sheep on that farmer/rancher's land, I was kicking and squirming and bleating my dissatisfaction. Something had changed in my life, and I didn't like it. Suddenly, I had found myself outside of my comfort zone, and I wanted people to know that I didn't like it. "The Lord is my Shepherd, and I'm about to be sheared," I said to my friend, looking up from my bowl of noodles.

"What's that?" he asked.

"Change," I said. "I can't control it, you can't control it, and it makes us feel uncomfortable sometimes. I guess God pulls us out of our comfort zones, and he has his own good reasons. We may not understand what he's trying to accomplish, and maybe we never will. But we have to trust that whatever he allows to happen will work to his own good purpose. It's like a sheep being sheared," I explained. "We may put up a fuss, but that uncomfortable feeling is all part of what makes us grow and fulfill our purpose."

"That's right," my friend said. "Now let me ask you this: How come you can tell sheep and duck stories, but when I want to draw an analogy from the wind, you don't want anything to do with it?"

"Sorry about that," I apologized. "Really, the wind story was very good. It led to a real breakthrough moment for me."

"Eat your noodles," he said.

God never promised that this Christian walk would come easy. In fact, his Word provides many examples of how difficult it can be. I always expected my progress would be measured in one direction, but the truth is that my walk consists of steps forward that mark progress and steps back that signify defeats. It is only by God's grace that the steps forward outnumber the steps back.

For it is God who works in you to will and to act according to his good purpose. Do everything without complaining or arguing, so that you may become blameless and pure, children of God without fault in a crooked and depraved generation, in which you shine like stars in the universe.

Philippians 2:13–15